AN EMOTIONAL
FIRST
AID KIT
FOR MOTHERS

AN EMOTIONAL FIRST AID KIT FOR MOTHERS

LINDA J. EYRE,
Margaret Archibald, Earlene Blaser,
Barbara Timothy Bowen, Ann Whiting Orton

BOOKCRAFT
Salt Lake City, Utah

Library of Congress Catalog Card Number: 97-71035
ISBN 1-57008-313-4

First Printing, 1997

Printed in the United States of America

To our fellow strugglers

Contents

Preface

Mothers. The word conjures up visions of the great care-giver, the healer, the soother, and the comforter. To a child she is one who can take the sting out of a scrape with a kiss, the throb out of a bump with a hug, and the cutting edge off of a disaster—like unkind words from a friend—with a sympathetic smile. Somehow mothers are the ones who are always expected to administer the first aid, make the chicken soup, deliver the casserole. However, there comes a time in every mother's life when *she* is the one who needs the aid.

"Be prepared," we always say as we tuck the first-aid kit into a son's pack for a fifty-mile hike. It contains an assortment of bandages—from Band-Aids for scrapes and small cuts to butterfly bandages for open slices and Ace bandages for sprains. Also found is antibiotic cream for unexpected infections, vitamin C in case of the warning signals of a cold, and tweezers for those pesky slivers. Painkillers are also included to take care of a wide range of discomfort, and maybe even a little snake-bite antidote in case of that unthinkable disaster. Like a good mother, we try to think of every conceivable problem a hike can pose, short of an earthquake, to include in this adventuresome son's first-aid kit.

"What about a first-aid kit for mothers?" I asked myself as I drove home after speaking to a large group of mothers. I had felt a great bond with these women as we had talked together about the challenges of being a mother. After my talk, mother after mother came to tell me about the difficulty of their lives. One said, "I have four children under five, and of all the things I've lost I miss my mind the most." Another confided, "I have a husband who is almost impossible to deal with," and another with tears about to spill over the edges of her eyes said, "My husband left me with five children who adore him, for another woman." Still others said things like: "I just feel so helpless. No matter how hard I try to be organized, my children seem to find ways to unorganize me!" "My son is threatening to leave home." "I have twelve children and my husband lost his job two years ago. I've been working from 11:00 P.M. until 5:00 A.M. since then to try to make ends meet." "My needs are different because I have a disabled child with so many special needs." Each needed her own kind of first aid to ease the pain. Motherhood is the greatest hike of all time, and I had just been faced with myriad disasters that mothers had encountered on their adventures—without much first aid. When they hand you that beautiful pink or blue bundle in the hospital, they don't include an instruction manual.

Often desperate single mothers plead with me to write a book for them, to which I always reply, "*You* have to write that book! I have not had your experiences—no one can really empathize with those singularly difficult needs unless you've been one." Speech after speech, face after face, and letter after letter over many years have convinced me that what mothers really need is a little first aid for themselves, an arm around their shoulder from someone who can say, "I know how you feel. This is what I learned when that very thing happened to me."

There is intense training and peer support for every exciting career except for the most important one—motherhood, that career that directs the course of lives forever. Yet it is hard for anyone to feel that they are a "mothering expert." Although, after years of experience, I might know just the thing to help with some cuts and bruises, and I was certainly good at telling mothers which trail *not* to take on their hike because of all the mistakes I'd made by traveling there, there is no way that I could put in all the necessary first-aid items for those who were taking different hikes and would run into different mountains and cliffs. So I began to collect friends with their own first-aid expertise. They had known the trials of many trails that I had never experienced. Each had collected "merit badges" in their own way. All have collected valuable knowledge from years of training by the best teachers—their children—as well as from the well-known and reliable "School of Hard Knocks."

When Margaret Archibald and I first began thinking about this project several years ago, we collected a group of young mothers who could help us remember the burning questions and concerns of young motherhood. As I then looked back to my own years as a young mother with several small children, I remembered so clearly the feeling that I was spending every day dealing with crisis after crisis. And so many failures, so many things went wrong. Every day I kept wishing that I could afford to hire a consultant to follow me around and tell me how to be more efficient, how to be a better cheerleader for the children, and how to quit making the same mistakes over and over again.

Even though the contributing writers-mothers for this book can't do that, we realized as we talked to young mothers, as well as more experienced mothers, that sometimes the best thing you can have in your mothering career is access to help from someone further along the trail of motherhood. Maybe by tucking this first-aid kit into your own backpack we can help you be a little more prepared and maybe even ease a little of the pain and guilt that are inevitable components of the hike. You'll hear about their joys and sorrows, successes and failures, and learn what they wished they had known. Just knowing that others know how you feel, have weathered the storms, have thought the same thoughts, and have not only learned a lot from the turbulence of life but at some point have also actually become grateful for it—this has got to be at least as good as Neosporin!

And now a brief word about how this book is organized. Each writer-mother has her own section wherein she describes the challenges and rewards of her life. At each section's beginning you will find a biographical note on that writer. As you read each chapter you will see that each of us has experienced different challenges and disasters, but the joy in the experience is the same. Interestingly, none of us have found the finishing line for this hike. In fact we have all found that not only does this mothering adventure never end but also it gets bigger and more exciting!

Of course, some needs are beyond us and require a higher aid from those who love us most and know us best, they from whom all aid and blessings flow, our loving Heavenly Father and our Savior Jesus Christ. They are the ones who know the profound importance of our partnerships with our mates and our stewardship over these magnificent people called our children, to whom we are entrusted in this greatest of all life's experiences: motherhood!

Linda Eyre
1997, Salt Lake City, Utah

P.S.

As reader and/or purchaser of this book it is appropriate for you to know that all the royalties will be going to a special charitable foundation and will be used to assist families in teaching values, in character education, and in mother training.

Introduction of Aid Givers

Though you will be more formally introduced to the women who have contributed to this book later in the text, I (Linda) want to tell you a little about how these five women—some of whom, until last year, were total strangers—have become dear friends. As I was pondering the need for this book, I realized immediately that there was no way that I could give breadth and depth to "first aid" needs beyond my own realm. Every mother is born with a specific set of genes and has grown up in a distinct environment. When I speak to mothers, I try to remember to preface all my remarks by reminding audiences that each person is married (or not) to a very different individual and has been blessed with children who each deal with life in their own peculiar (or should I say particular?) way. Everyone has different coping skills, everyone has different needs, everyone sees life through their own window. I love the quote by Anaïs Nin, "We don't see things as they are. We see things as we are."

Because of that I knew that we needed mothers with a much wider spectrum than I could provide with only one strange but wonderful husband and nine types of children. In order to administer first aid, I felt I needed to find mothers who had had real experience with injuries and maladies and who had real problems and knew how to administer real salves and remedies. I also believe that sometimes the greatest remedy can be just knowing that someone has been through what you have and has survived.

1

I began my search thinking of women I have known and admired not only because of their unique gifts but especially because of how they have handled horrendous and harried, gory and grueling, common and uncommon difficulties in their lives.

For years Margaret and I have been talking about writing a book together. Having been friends since we met in Boston while our husbands were attending the Harvard Business School in 1970, we have been talking about our mothering dilemmas as well as the needs of other struggling mothers every time we could catch up with each other amidst multitudes of moves and life's complications. Having raised her seven incredible sons and a delightful daughter in the mission field as well as so capably handling the responsibilities of being the wife of a hyperactive, type A, CEO husband who is now also a bishop, I knew she could handle anything!

Ann recently moved into our ward as she entered a new marriage and brought such a spirit of love and kindness as well as wonderful, kind, and enthusiastic children. Having come through a devastating divorce and the accompanying complications so gracefully, besides being a well-known journalist, made her a perfect addition for the needs of single mothers as well as multiple other quandaries.

Earlene and her husband have been great friends of mine since our days together at Utah State University. My wonder at her enthusiasm, leadership abilities, and great sense of humor has been magnified a hundredfold as I have watched her deal with the seemingly insurmountable difficulties of raising eight children, one of whom she was told would not live for eight months. Eighteen years later she has rarely had a full night's sleep and is dealing with saving this son's life daily with unimaginable complications. In spite of it all, I always look forward to her hilarious Christmas letter as she continues to raise truly amazing kids.

Barbara came to us by inspiration. Richard and I came to know her through her new husband, Gordon Bowen, who has been a dear friend, stimulator, and creator of wonderful ideas

in our lives for many years. Her ability to use her phenome-
nal spiritual strength to get through the difficulty of many
years of surviving hard times, then losing her husband to
brain cancer, was more than an inspiration. It was enlighten-
ment, as we watched her deal with trials you will begin to
understand as you read her chapters. One day as I was rack-
ing my brain for one more element that we needed to complete this book, Gordon called. I am convinced that it was
more than a coincidence.

The love we feel for each other has grown in a truly
unique way. Two of the mothers live on the east coast and
three in the Salt Lake City area at the moment. We've enjoyed two lunches with different combinations of four of us
and have never really all been together except on two conference calls when we all got on the phone at the same time for
an hour. Though I have known everyone, Barbara and Margaret have never met, and the others have only "touched
spirits" for an hour or two. But we have learned to love and
admire and empathize with each through our writing. As you
read on, you will see what we mean.

I learned several major insights as I read the inner
struggles and dilemmas of motherhood presented by each
mother; the first being how different all our lives are, even
though there are many similarities. During our first conference call, as I was laughing about feeling that I would never,
never, NEVER get to the end of all the things that needed to
be done to keep all nine of our children rolling along, Barbara
confided that she had always planned to have twelve children but that was not to be her lot. After many heartaches
with miscarriages and infertility, she was padding around in
a house with only two of her three children, aching for the
commotion and pandemonium of a house full of rowdy bodies.
What an interesting process it is to deal with what the Lord
has dealt us, planned or not!

As I read Ann's chapters, I learned so much about compassion for those who are in different situations than mine.
Previously I had no idea of the complications and entangle-

ments of being a single, divorced mother with children. A new light dawns on the difficulties of all single mothers as they are faced with the dilemmas of emotions all the way around and even the horrible thought of dating again. I also realized why she was always the first to show up at my door when we were in need of help with Eagle projects or service projects of any kind in the ward.

The sum and substance of what wise Earlene has to say, not only about raising her children but especially about dealing with a severely disabled child, gives me new insight and strength to go on when I think my life is hard. It also helps me realize why she has a special light . . . a unique polish . . . that comes only from living through trials such as she has endured with grace and humor.

Although I learned many things from Margaret's chapter that I thought I knew, I want to thank her from the bottom of my heart for finally helping me feel good about my teenagers sleeping in church and for reminding me in her chapter on "Looking Back" that no two children ever have the same parents!

Barbara offered me a new way to empathize with those going through difficulties beyond their control. I learned new insights, new ways to understand, relief in knowing that someone else feels like I do, and pleasure in learning how to rely on the Lord with a smile in the face of tragedy. I watched her struggle with writing about painful things in her life and encouraging others of us to enjoy the therapy of writing about wretchedness.

I think we all learned that there is more than one way to be a good mother. We laughed together about our differences in the way we disciplined kids and what we considered "okay." What we realized is that there may be different methods, different kids, and different parents—all with the same result if sensitivity, communication, and a genuine commitment to do our best is in place, even though our best may not be perfect. The book gives a picture of things as we see them. Of course, we don't claim to be right about everything.

The last insight that we all learned in this process is that there is no way to address all the difficulties that mothers face. There are a multitude of complicated issues that we could only touch on or put off until a future book or request that you turn over to a bona fide physician. Some problems need the help of a medical expert; and once again we remember that all our "medical" needs, in the end, must be turned over to the Great Physician, the only one who can truly give us rest.

As mentioned earlier, each contributing mother has written her own section of this book describing things she has learned and experienced in her own adventure so far. To help you find the first-aid needs that are most important to you at the moment, chapter subtitles are shown on the contents page.

We present his book to you—a great mother in your own right—as we all strive to raise these Stripling Warriors, this Royal Army which includes the great leaders of a generation which could very well usher in the Second Coming of our Savior. We offer it with a figurative warm hug and smile and with the hope and prayer that our efforts will help heal the wounds just a little, salve your heart just a bit, and revitalize your appreciation for the magnificent blessing of being a mother.

Barbara Timothy Bowen

Barbara Boyce Timothy Bowen was born in Salt Lake City in 1950 to wonderful parents who were wise enough to not give her a middle name (but *to* give her a birth year from which she could always easily calculate her age). She loved the stage. Somewhat shy by nature, on stage she could assume the confidence of any character and live in the world of song and dance. She followed these interests through college, but a ski injury while training for the University of Utah ski team detoured her to Brigham Young University where she obtained a composite major in music, theater, and psychology.

After serving an LDS mission to the New England states, she returned to BYU and obtained a master's degree in communications. At this time she met Steven D. Timothy, who was on his way to Colorado State University. They were married in 1976 and spent the next seven years in Colorado, where Steve studied veterinary medicine and Barbara did graduate work in marriage and family therapy. When they moved back to Salt Lake City, Barbara was a practicing therapist through Valley Mental Health and LDS Social Services.

After their third son was born, Steve was diagnosed with a malignant brain tumor. He continued to practice for six more years. In 1993, Steve took the family on a sabbatical to Scotland; he died nine months after their return.

The next year challenged Barbara as she cared for her sons, an exchange student, and other youth who were drawn to her home. In 1995 she married her friend since high school, Gordon Bowen.

Who's Writing This Script, Anyway?

Ophthalmic ointment for those whose lives are not what they'd envisioned

I am not a master mother. I am a muddling, struggling, befuddled mother whose chapters for this book have been scrawled on pieces of crumpled paper while waiting in the emergency room, scribbled on events schedules at track meets, and, recently, scratched on one son's form for camp while sitting in the shade of an old baseball dugout waiting for another son to finish a tennis match.

They have been written from the back bedroom where I've been mending after major orthopedic surgery, in a home whose counters and floors are filled with the wreckage and treasures of life as we tear apart our house in preparation to move across the country, written as I'm still mourning the death of my first husband while beginning life with a dear new husband whose intense job (and my desire to let my senior in high school complete his last year) has required us to live 2000 miles apart. They have been written through days of tears, mostly my own, when I felt like a failure as a mother. Yesterday, I lay face down in the middle of the kitchen floor, like our 13-year-old dog does, to see if any of the children would notice. My youngest son just stepped over me. Later he told me he thought I was napping!

These chapters were not written with a "how to" approach, as in how to increase children's responsibility and laundry efficiency by having them pin their dirty, mated socks together and wash them in a mesh bag. There will be no "how-to's," only views, on motherhood and life, mostly because I still don't know "how-to" (and I'd like to meet the mother who gets her children to pin their dirty socks together at the end of each day), and because what has helped me the most in mothering has not been the list from someone else of what to do, but rather a reconsideration of how I view this role, the windows through which I look at this enormous, challenging and also wonderful experience. And while I have been writing these chapters, I find comfort in knowing that the best writer, the True Author of our lives, is continuing to write the next chapters of my life. I just need the courage to show up for the part.

It's one of those days. It feels like one of those lives. The oatmeal burned this morning while you were trying to find an Indian costume for your second grader. Your junior high school student forgot to set his alarm again (has he ever set it?), so now you need to drive him because he missed the car pool, and your fifth grader is pleading for you to fix the zipper on his backpack and provide some fast information on blue whales so he can write a report before the bus comes. There's no milk. Your second grader is at the sink filling his bowl of cornflakes with water, still in hopes of a fine breakfast.

Minutes later you return from a frantic trip to the junior high with a bowl of oatmeal mush plastered to the inside of the passenger door (did you really think you could camouflage the taste with enough maple syrup?). But you're relieved that your two youngest children have made it to the bus, even if one did forget his lunch, the other his saxophone. It's okay. You have to go to their school in fifteen minutes anyway to meet with your child's teacher, school counselor, and psychologist to discuss your youngest student's prognosis.

You arrive late to the conference (because your car is stalling again) but in time to be informed that your child tests high but performs low and has not sat still or quit talking since he entered the school two years ago. They suggest a psychiatrist and perhaps Ritalin. This is the news you have to deliver to your husband at your next stop at the University Hospital. He has been there for two days to receive an experimental chemotherapy in his fight against cancer.

You're glad to see he's awake and not vomiting. You feed him from the lunch tray, try to give him some encouragement and comfort, report on the morning's events, and then spread out the bills on the bed so you can discuss them. You're trying to be a loving wife, speaking in soft supportive tones, when you find an unexpected bill and shriek, "What's this?" As the nurse exits, she asks you to kindly not upset her patient. You apologize, then swallow hard as you realize that your part-time work as a marriage and family therapist will have to become more full-time. More clients. More problems. At least their problems help you forget your own.

Using the hospital phone, you make an appointment for your car to be looked at since it's leaking oil, make a call to the dishwasher repairman, and then log several more calls to reschedule your clients. You kiss your sleeping husband good-bye, go pick up the car pool, and take the boys to swimming lessons. No one wants to go, but you decided when your middle son lost most of the vision in one eye that a sport which didn't require depth-of-field vision would be ideal. Of course, he's the child who likes it the least and is the one who lost his goggles and fins at the pool last week, so first you have to go through the dressing rooms downstairs at the pool to reach the lost and found.

The stairs cause that sharp pain in your knees to shout for attention, but who has time for knees with demanding kids everywhere you turn and a husband in the hospital? You console yourself with the thought that you'll address the problem the next time you're at the emergency room with one of the boys. (You know you won't have to wait long because visits come weekly.) Just then, a high school boy above you in the stairwell decides to relieve his nasal passages on a friend below and misses. You pretend nothing hit you, but your son asks what is on your face. It's not so bad, but today is your birthday, and you were hoping for a little nicer day, a little more consideration, a little nicer gift. Then suddenly excavating to the bottom of the box of moldy towels and tangled goggles, you find the swimsuit and one fin. Life is looking up!

Life is *definitely* looking up. You return home and find that your neighbor has left you a birthday cake and a small gift. However, your golden retriever has also left you a gift—the remains of a dead quail under the table, probably in exchange for the hefty bite of cake she took. But at least now the kids remember it's your birthday, and maybe they'll be more helpful. You make a festive dinner—four pieces of pizza left over from last night, a few leaves of lettuce, wreckage from the birthday cake—and then you all pile in the car to go see Dad.

After a fight for the front seat, a request to go to the library first, and four serious attempts at starting the car, it's evident that you're going to spend the evening at home. It's then the regular nightly scramble of homework; arguments over who doesn't want to feed the dog, who doesn't want to take a bath, who doesn't want to do the dishes (especially fervent tonight since the dishwasher's broken); and a phone call to the hospital so each child can report how exceptionally well he's doing and say good-night to Dad.

Finally, you fall into bed. Then you remember the gift with your birthday cake. Removing the birthday wrappings reveals a videotape with a small note lauding this as the best movie ever made, a 4-star masterpiece not to be missed that will make you laugh and cry and will change your life forever. Tired as you are, this sounds worth watching. And, after all, it *is* your birthday. So you pop it into the VCR and crawl back into bed with great anticipation

The opening scene pulls you into a crowded school auditorium where the camera focuses on the faces of a beautiful family nestled together, listening admiringly to their oldest son deliver the valedictorian address at graduation. Radiant faces. The husband gently places his arm around his wife and whispers thanks to her for raising such an outstanding child. She smiles, knowing how much their son has been guided and influenced by a brilliant and loving father. You feel the lump in your throat as you reflect on your own family situation and picture your husband in the hospital.

You learn that the father is an eminent cardiologist who is praised by his colleagues and patients and widely revered for his remarkable innovations in his field. The mother is an extremely successful interior designer who also devotes much energy to important social causes at home and abroad, which has made her a key figure in the community. These are strong, vibrant, healthy people—of ideal weight and perfect figures—who love each other and their children. *Their children!* Wonderful, rosy-cheeked children who excel in all they do.

You feel the pain well up in your heart as you compare this family's life to your own disheveled existence. You watch scene after scene of accomplishments—the youngest daughter attends the Junior Olympics in gymnastics and earns a gold medal; one of the sons wins the Young Inventors award and is honored in Washington, D.C. All the children practice the piano; brush their teeth; have no acne, learning disabilities, or insecurities; seem to truly care about each other; and cooperate to get the housework and yardwork done.

You watch as perfectly preened cars pull into the driveway of a lovely home where, once inside, you find exquisite design and perfect order. There are no scuff marks on the walls or toothpaste on the bathroom mirrors. No toilet would think of flooding here. In this home, everything glistens. Each evening, the family gathers for dinner—always a nutritious, well-balanced, aesthetically pleasing meal—graciously set at the dining room table, which is graciously adorned with flowers from their stunning English flower garden. Between well-mannered bites, they converse about the day's events, personal feelings, and international affairs and deftly discuss goals and means for self-improvement while learning three new vocabulary words and the presidents of the United States.

After several more scenes of spectacular vacations, genuine acts of social service, perfect parties for which each of the children performs, scenes where the mother receives an honorary doctorate concurrent with being named mother of the year, more awards, more perfectly hedged gardens, and many moments of marital and family harmony—after all this, the show finally ends.

You sit up in bed and hear yourself say, "What kind of story was that? Nothing happened. Absolutely nothing!" You are completely perplexed as to how this inane script could have been made into a movie, puzzled as to how your friend could possibly have seen merit in such an insipid story, and angry at yourself for having wasted your time watching it. But something good must have come from it because, after haranguing over the stupidity of this movie, you begin to review your own tangled and troubled life, and as you fall asleep that night . . . you smile.

Think about it. If we could have the kind of life we often wish for—especially as mothers living in stress, chaos, and endless problems yet wanting the perfect life of no pain, no obstacles, and children who only excel—and if this life were then made into a movie, you can bet that people would walk out of it and demand their money back. If the continual success story we would write for ourselves were published in a book, it would get horrible reviews; if anyone were actually willing to suffer through to the end, she'd either throw the book across the room in frustration or sit dazed, wondering why in the world such a boring story was ever put into print.

I don't mean that we don't need a vision of how we'd like our lives to be. As mothers, we absolutely need dreams to build on, but we must also understand that the real richness and meaning of life come from the plethora of problems inherent in motherhood. We might argue that if we could write the script for our own life, we'd help all the suffering children in orphanages, fight for world peace, discover a cure for cancer, and raise outstanding children who would make major contributions to society. All well and good, but our story would still be uninspiring because we would choose to not include the pain. How could we? It's against human nature to wish for it. Who would write in divorce, multiple sclerosis, or bankruptcy? Would anyone write cancer into her story, or rape, or life in a wheelchair? Who would choose to include depression or the death of a spouse or a child? Some might have the courage to include fighting a cold or dealing with car troubles, but most wouldn't because who wants even *those* problems!

The truth is, God is the best author of our lives. He is an exquisite writer and writes for each of us an incredible script with complex twists and turns. He has not only the courage to include the pain but also the insight to choose carefully and specifically the trials and problems each of us needs to make a profound and soul-stirring story. If a famous director or author were to walk through your door today with a request to do the story of your life, rest assured that you would have ample material for an incredible film or book. You would not need to have climbed Mount Everest, been the First Lady, or won a Nobel Prize. Just going through the day-to-day struggles of being alive is wonderment and story enough. But get ready! As you view life in this way, you begin to relish your trials and see the spectrum from frustration to devastation not as hardship but as *abundant good material!*

As a note, the birthday story in the beginning of this chapter was my actual fortieth birthday, except there was no videotape at the end of the day to help me compare the craziness of my life to what I thought was the perfect life. Had there been, I might have realized that mine was much richer and much funnier. As I used to tuck in my middle child, he would look up at me and, with a slight lisp, say, "Tell me your goodths, your badths, and your funnyths." It was our nightly ritual. He'd tell me his, I'd tell him mine, and at the end he'd invariably say, "Mom, you juths don't have enough funnyths in your life!" It was true. I was seeing the seriousness and the heartache but missing the humor, so I began to notice what was funny so I'd have something to laugh about with him each night. And, in the process, I began to see many of my "bads" as "funnies."

James Thurber said that true humor "is emotional chaos remembered in tranquility." Mothers have a profusion of emotional chaos and, therefore, an abundance of humorous material, or "funnies," like the time my sweet children skipped happily into the house with a lovely yellow necklace of leaves made just for me. How could they have known it was poison oak and that I'd look like a victim of Chernobyl, with open, oozing sores, for weeks after? Or when, as poor students, we were only able to afford a party line, and I received a very reprimanding call from the phone company threatening to discontinue our service because of a reported "heavy breather" traced to our house. They didn't believe it was my one-year-old, Adam, who loved to grab the phone from his high chair and listen but who just hadn't learned to talk yet!

After seeming catastrophes, when things finally calm down, it's not difficult to look at the moments of chaos turned to humor and accept them as good material. Comedy is easy. Tragedy is harder. Even if we had the insight to include the daily devastations as part of a good story, we would never include tragedy. Heartache is not funny. But heartache weaves its way through each of our lives and gives each life its strongest, richest fiber. Yet when we're experiencing the sorrow, we feel somehow that our life is wrong. I believe most people would say that their lives are not the way they would have written them. Some may be close, but most lives encounter so many lost dreams and disappointments—so many trials, twists, and turns—that people often feel they've been cast into someone else's play, portraying someone else's story.

My life is not how I would have written it. I dreamed about a life more like the one in the movie with a husband who was continually strong, supportive, and healthy and an abundance of adorable children. By the time I was nine, I had names for all 12 of the children I wanted—10 boys and 2 girls (aware of my inability to fix hair, I limited the number of girls). I spent many happy days imagining all the activities and exchanges in our home. I saw myself and my husband in a great team effort to raise this large family of accomplished children and together make a significant contribution to the community.

After a mission and a master's degree I married, at age 26, someone four years younger than myself who had only one year of his undergraduate degree. By this time I had reduced the number of desired children to 7 (I kept the ones with the best names), but I felt confident that my story was beginning to unfold just as I had dreamed. I couldn't have known what chapters God had in mind. Had I read them in advance, I would have shut the book and said that he must have mixed me up with someone else. Either that or he needed a better editor.

I couldn't have known how hard it would be to get the three sons I have to this earth—the infertility, the miscarriages, the interminable medical procedures, and the endless unconsoled tears. I would never have planned on a husband who suffered from depression, struggled in school, and had to war with and eventually die from a malignant brain tumor. I wouldn't have written in a child with a rare eye disease that impaired his vision, or another child who was bright but every year struggled so in school. I wouldn't have included any of the loneliness or heartache. I would have written a much different story.

But without those problems I wouldn't have cheered and praised the heavens when my husband finally graduated from veterinary school and built a national award-winning animal hospital. I wouldn't have rejoiced when our son who had weathered three eye surgeries became our best tennis player, and our son who had struggled to remember the months of the year memorized and performed, flawlessly, eight pages of a script. I wouldn't have known the tenderness in caring for someone who is dying nor wept to see the pure and childlike spirit emerging in a man who was full of love for all of us. I wouldn't have known the depths. I wouldn't have known the heights. And I wouldn't have known that I was part of a perfect story.

One early spring, exhausted, discouraged, in need of
restoration and renewed meaning in life, I retreated to our
little family cabin in Wildwood. After two days I had fed the
deer that had graced my door, walked through snowy paths
under a star-filled sky, read, prayed, cried, and sat quietly
next to the blazing fire, but I had not found the answers I
was seeking. Then one morning, as I lay in bed, not asleep
but not yet awake, gazing at the ceiling, the rafters above me
opened, and I began viewing scenes from my early married
life as vividly as if I were seated in the theatre.

I watched myself juggle my first baby, his carrier, bouncy
chair, bag of toys, diapers, bottles, and other accoutrements
three miles across campus because I didn't have a car, but I
did have a secretarial job for $3.35 an hour where I learned
the art of typing while nursing, fixing a bottle, and changing
a diaper. I was also there holding my screaming middle child
as my husband stitched his forehead for the fourth time that
year in our makeshift kitchen surgery suite.

I smelled the night air and felt my wearied body on the
many 2:00 A.M. stroller rides for my toddler who had night
terrors and, at age two, had not yet slept through the night.
And I watched us swelter in 105-degree summer heat for
three nights before we realized that our three-year-old had
added to the temperature when he turned on the electric
heat in the house (which we hardly did even in the winter because it was too expensive!).

I watched my two-year-old nearly run over me (and the
kindly man in the parking lot who was helping me look
under the hood of the old Toyota while it was running) when
he put the car into drive and it lunged 40 feet across the lot
and smashed into a new Cadillac. (I also reviewed the note I
left on their car saying my two-year-old was very sorry for
not driving more courteously.) I saw myself riding with my
husband on the way to a marriage seminar weekend, full of
anticipation for a renewed relationship, until I turned and
saw twenty veterinary books on the back seat, and he let me
know he was full of anticipation for a quiet place to study. I

saw myself clutch my baby, with a sinking feeling in my stomach, and hold tightly the hand of my four-year-old as we walked down rain-drenched streets trying to find their father, who should have been home hours earlier after having taken one of his most critical exams, which meant he was probably grieving somewhere because he had not passed.

I saw myself one summer fill the metal lunch box for my weary hard hat husband who was going to work every day at the copper mines, while I, in a continual state of nausea, substitute taught junior high students who threw chairs and classmates out of windows. My only joy was in our one-year-old son, and my hope was in the anticipation of this new baby inside me. Then I relived the long ride from Salt Lake City to Denver to attend a family wedding while I held onto the loops on either side of the car, the intense pain of premature labor gripping my body, while my little boy kept looking up and saying, "Mama sad?" The next day, my "hope" was delivered, 5 months early and lifeless.

And, more than once, I saw myself sobbing in the lonely car I'd driven to the mouth of the canyon so no one could hear me cry as the rain outside echoed my sorrow. There were many scenes too painful to recount here, but as scene upon scene flooded onto the screen above me that morning I laughed out loud, cried more than I have in any movie, and towards the end heard myself say, "It's perfect." I was surprised at those words, actually astounded, because to me my life had seemed anything but perfect. But it wasn't the perfection of the ideal family, where everything glistens, that was being portrayed here—it was God's kind of perfect.

Looking back on it now, it still seems like my life was, and is, a mess, but in that one moment I knew differently. In that one moment I knew that God was the author and that he was writing a marvelous, unsurpassed script with holy mirth and perfect pain, a story with great material, a story written just for me that would finally bring me back home. And I knew that, by the time I got there, I wouldn't ask for my money back.

My Mistake

Rx for the bumps and bruises
caused by our mistakes

I get angry. I make mistakes. I forget things. Unfortunately, it's not usually my mistakes that I forget.

My children lose things and break things and don't always measure up. We must be related. But I've come to understand that it's okay to be imperfect. Rudolph Dreikurs calls it "the courage to be imperfect." I like that. I think it does take courage—at least to admit that we're not. There was only One who was ever perfect.

Seven months pregnant and without a car, I strained as I peddled up the steep hill to take our first child to his summer activity program. I was pleased that they'd allow our not-yet-three-year-old to attend, feeling this was an important step in his socialization. But as I began riding home, I heard a plaintive exhausted cry. I stopped and saw my little Adam running towards me with the counselors from the program in fast pursuit of this frightened boy who clearly did not want to go to class that day. Given how much he normally ran away from home, I should have been glad he was running towards home, but as the counselors circled, all of my indignation came bursting forth, and I insisted that this weeping child return to class. In fact, I voiced my disappointment so vehemently, one would have thought this child had failed out of Harvard rather than just had a bad day at preschool!

Riding home *I* was the weeping child, confused as to why

it was so intensely important to me that my son succeed at his first structured social experience. Why did it matter? Yes, he was the first child, but he was still only a baby. Then, for just a moment, I remembered the little girl I had been, hiding behind the bed, crying, afraid to come out and play, and I knew that had much more to do with my insecurities than it had to do with his.

On Saturdays I used to take my boys—ages 8, 5, and 3—skiing, along with three of their friends. Invariably we would arrive just as the blizzard did, and it was chaos buckling six little pairs of boots and sorting through tangled skis, poles, hats, gloves, and goggles. Waiting in line for tickets one morning, while being blasted with icy gusts of wind, my middle son whined that his boots were too tight. I told him that ski boots always hurt, to just get used to it. Then I looked down and discovered I'd squeezed one of his feet into his younger brother's miniature boot, while the little brother was sloshing around in a boot three sizes too big. I apologized, exchanged their boots, and we laughed. All of this pandemonium was acceptable until my oldest son announced the unpardonable—he'd left one of his gloves at home. In that moment, I lost it. "How could you do that?!" I cried, as if he'd just driven the car full of kids and ski equipment off the nearest cliff. "How could you forget your glove? Why didn't you check before you left? I told you to check everything! What are we going to do now? You know you can't ski on a day this cold without a glove . . ." On and on I went in wrenching profusion about this glove.

After we were on the lift (my son's hand wrapped in someone's extra ski hat), I pulled my parka around my face to hide my shame and keep my tears from freezing. How could one forgotten ski glove have made me so angry? I thought about the moment with Adam at the preschool, years earlier, and the many other times since when my exasperation exceeded the incident. Why couldn't I be more patient? What was wrong with me? The answer came directly but mercifully. I wasn't really angry with my son at all—I was angry at myself, angry with the child in me who had gone through life forgetting and losing and breaking things.

How could I be angry with him? Wasn't I the one who had used my dad's best silver cufflinks for a costume and left them in the girls' restroom at school? Wasn't I the one who had borrowed my sister's purse in Hawaii and then left it on top of the car as we took off to tour the island? Wasn't I the one who, singing before two thousand high school students, forgot the words and ran off the stage crying? Wasn't I the one who always broke my zippers, knocked over my milk at dinner, and could never find anything because it was layered in a labyrinth of clothes, papers, and projects?

These foibles were not restricted to my youth. When my second baby was just a few weeks old, I bundled him in his baby carrier and, with his three-year-old brother, headed to the student bookstore to pick up some materials for classes I was taking. Purchases in hand, we returned home. Only as I was helping my little boy out of the car did the horrifying realization hit—I had left my baby on the counter in the bookstore! I ran into the house and made a frantic, fumbling call, "Excuse me but I, um, is there a—oh, please help me, I left my baby in the art supplies. Is he still there?" The laughter on the other end of the phone came as a great relief. It meant I hadn't lost my precious baby. I'd only lost my mind!

As I sat on that chairlift that morning, I was finally able to voice the truth—what bothered me about my children, or anyone else for that matter, was what bothered me about myself. It was a freeing thought. That night I told them, "From now on, remember this one thing: when I get angry with you, I'm really only angry with myself." They liked that idea. I did too. But it wasn't long before one of them did something that really upset me, and, as I was chasing him through the house, he looked over his shoulder and shouted, "Remember, you're only angry with yourself!" And I yelled back, "I'm not either, I'm angry with you!" But after I'd quieted down, the truth manifest itself again. I was yelling at the little girl inside of me, still castigating her for her mistakes. I just couldn't seem to forgive her for not being perfect.

Before I began my practice as a marriage and family therapist I was only vaguely aware of the child inside of me. But in working through the multitudinous problems and pain of others, she became very real. When I discovered her, she was about five years old and had been figuratively left in a closet for many years, crying and angry. Nurturing and loving this child has been prerequisite to being able to nurture and love my own children, every client who stepped through my door, or any other person who came into my life.

I had to learn to accept this little girl with all her faults, just the way she was. I had to accept myself, become more real as a person, and not worry about my image as an all-knowing, wise therapist. I had to not worry about my image at all. My children helped me with this on numerous occasions, especially when my clients would call me at home with problems that came up during the week. But it seemed whenever my clients needed me, my children needed me more. As soon as I got on the phone they'd attach themselves to the other end of the 40 feet of coiled cord and start winding up in it like a human top until the phone was jerked out of my hand and flung into the wall.

If I sought seclusion by stretching the cord across the kitchen to the tiny bathroom, I'd have to wedge the phone between my shoulder and my ear so I could grab the door knob with both hands in a grueling effort to keep the door shut while my boys pulled with all their might to get it open, pounding, crying, and fighting on the other side. Invariably the client would stop their stream of disclosure and say, "Do you need some help?" I did! But how could I ask *them?* The truth is, it was good for them to see the marriage and family therapist struggling with her own family. Somehow, when my professional image was blown, they had more hope for themselves. And I had more hope for myself. It allowed me to begin to accept my weaknesses and the little girl inside me with all of hers.

Sometime ago I placed on my mantel a picture of the Savior and later leaned next to it a portrait photo of myself as a two and a half year old, bright-eyed and looking towards him. It wasn't until I added another picture—Jesus surrounded by the little children—that I began thinking of myself in that setting and wondered if I would have been one of those to sit on his lap. At first, as much as I wanted him to take me in his arms like the happy children in front of me, I stood far away in the shadows, unsure he could love me and be forgiving of my mistakes. Yet, passing by those pictures each day, I could feel myself coming a timid step closer.

The truth is, as I've become more accepting of myself my children have too. And they've also become better at not taking me too seriously when I do get angry, routinely reminding me that I'm only angry with myself. My oldest son is so well trained that recently, after having railed on him for something, I apologized sincerely, and his cheerful response was, "Oh, that's okay. I knew you weren't really angry with me, so I didn't listen to anything you said." My middle son deftly cut me off at the pass as I was about to explode over having to make my eighth trip to the school that day, this time to look for his shin guards that he'd left on the soccer field. Before I could say one word, he looked at me and remarked, "You know, Mom, the reason I do these things is because subconsciously I just want to spend more time with you."

And the youngest, who is often in trouble and therefore often subject to getting yelled at for his mistakes, learned early on how to dissuade my anger. After doing something intolerable when he was little, he'd look at me with those sweet, sparkling eyes and say, "I no naughty. I nice." Or in the middle of my hot pursuit, he'd say, "I wuv you so much. Say dat to me." Not long ago, as I marched up the stairs, scowling and ready to let Eric have it for some misdeed, he looked up from underneath the covers and began singing, "Mother dear, I love you so, your happy smiling face . . ." Before he could get to "is such a joy to look at," my face *was* smiling.

Sometimes, I still forget. I got upset both times my son

shattered the glass on the rear window of the van, even though I was the first one who had hurriedly and absent-mindedly backed out of the driveway one day with the hatch raised wide open, causing a cascade of glass to pour inside the car and on the meal I was taking some lucky person. My son was quick to remind me that I was only upset because I'd done the same thing. I told him it was true. I have learned to admit when I'm wrong. What I didn't know how to do was face the guy at the glass company for the third time in three months. As I was paying for that third sheet of glass, he asked me if I wanted to schedule ahead for next month, and I actually considered it!

But sometimes, I remember. The day my son's friend drove right through our garage door, taking out the whole door and part of the house with him, I didn't get upset. In fact, when I drove up and saw those two boys desperately trying to sweep up the rubble of mangled metal and bungled brick, I could only laugh. The boy felt terrible. For some reason, I only felt love. Later, after watching him play a football game, I sent him some cookies and a kind of thank you note, telling him he was a tremendous young man with the ability to make great impact.

I have learned from many people about parenting, patience, and acceptance of mistakes. One of the best teachers has been my mother-in-law, who went through the trenches as a mother to my first husband. Steve had such delightful but mischievous creative energy, she had to be even more creative, and he was often put on a long dog leash connected to the clothesline to keep him out of trouble. One day, when she thought he was taking his afternoon nap, she got a call from a neighbor saying that he must have escaped through the window because he had mounted one of the giant tractors while the workmen were at lunch and was just now driving down the street!

She always loved the little boy in Steve and the child in all of us, having been a school teacher for 20 years, and that love came without judgment. The year we lived with her and Adam spilled a gallon of red Kool-Aid, ruining her beige kitchen carpet, her cheerful response was, "Oh good, now I can get tile!"

Another person from whom I've learned much about parenting came as somewhat of a surprise. Because he had no children of his own, I thought I would be the one to gently teach my present husband about raising children. Not so. Every day, I am taught by this wise and loving man.

Eric said to me one evening, "When's Gordon coming home? I can't wait. He always sees the good in me." I think that must be Gordon's secret.

Certainly, he knows they have faults. He knows they make mistakes, and he will keep me awake at night discussing concerns he has for each of the boys. But for him, every weakness is only a potential strength, every strength is celebrated, and he values whatever is important to them.

One night, after a grueling week and one more 2000-mile flight home, he dropped, exhausted. I was having a party for Adam that night, and Eric was having a sleepover, so he might have rested but when Collin walked in bored, Gordon sat up suddenly and said, "Collin, whatever you want to do tonight, I'm up for it." Collin's quick reply was . . . bungee jumping—which they did!

And last week, home sick with the flu, instead of going to bed he ate his chicken noodle soup while letting Eric use an entire roll of duct tape to bind him to the chair, then spent an hour and a half struggling to get out of the fearsome confines while Eric laughed. Gordon's quiet comment was: "It's okay. I think it's Eric's way of showing affection." He loves the child in all of us. I know he loves the little girl in me.

One Sunday afternoon I took each of my sons aside and, after a prayer, I played a small video segment of each of them as a little boy. I felt this was especially important for my oldest son, who would soon be off to college and who had grown up so quickly when his father was diagnosed with cancer ten years ago. "Imagine this is your little boy," I said, "because he is and always will be. Tell me, what would you teach him? What would you feed him? How would you care for this little boy?" I also had them close their eyes and imagine talking and playing with the child.

My younger sons could easily visualize the little boy and describe what they felt about him and what they wanted for him. But my oldest son struggled to imagine this little child and finally said: "I can't; it's too hard for me." I cried inside. Adam, who had been the most vibrant, life-filled little boy, had become such a handsome, good young man. He had excelled academically. He had learned to play the piano with sensitivity and rugby with fervor. But where had he left the little boy?

After a summer in New Zealand and Israel and six weeks into college, Adam came to visit. When we had a minute to talk, he said: "At first I only wanted to be the warrior for rugby. But in Israel, I thought about the little boy. I missed him. I decided I wanted to be better friends, so I took him by the hand and talked with him. Then I only wanted to be the little kid.

"One morning in Israel," he continued, "the most powerful image came. I pictured myself as a child at the feet of the Savior. I was so small, I was sitting down hugging his leg. Suddenly I felt these loving hands pick me up and hold me next to Him. I knew in that moment that He had never let me go and would not through all eternity."

I am still making mistakes. Yesterday, I forgot to pick up my fifteen-year-old from the high school, and he waited an hour before finding a ride. Certain that he would be angry, I apologized profusely when I saw him later that day. He just looked at me and said, "What do you mean, Mom? You *did* pick me up. You just forgot!" I checked my memory before I laughed at his humorous pardon of my mistake.

Yesterday I also discovered that he'd deleted the spell check, grammar check, and thesaurus features from the word processor on our computer. For a second I thought about being angry, but how could I? Why should I? It was, after all, only a mistake. I've come to appreciate that on this earth there has only been one perfect person, and right now I choose to be just a little child sitting in His lap.

Running Away, Running Home

Soothing salve for mothers who want their children
to be independent but don't want to let go

When my children were little, they liked to run away.
I don't mean once in a while; I mean every time there was an
open door or a hole in the fence, they were gone. I guess I
should say my children *loved* to run away.

As pajama-clad toddlers, they would slip out of the house
only to be returned by trembling motorists. They would escape from the watchful eyes of the nursery leaders at church
and be found playing happily on the busy boulevard. Or they
would be discovered (thanks to a trail of tiny abandoned
clothes) splashing happily in the creek, when I thought they
were inside napping. At age two, our son Adam disappeared
so suddenly while shopping one afternoon for clothes with his
grandparents that they thought he had been abducted. A
panicked search ensued throughout the department store
until finally they located him in the baby furniture section,
snuggled in a comfy crib, sound asleep!

For this very reason, I did not take a nap for two and a
half years after my last baby, Eric, was born—at least not
while he was awake. (Eric was always awake.) But on one
particular spring afternoon, as my body was wilting from exhaustion, I decided maybe, just maybe, I could chance it.
After all, I had put strong locks on the gates outside, nailed
the garage door opener high out of reach, and installed heavy
bolts at the tops of all the doors that led to freedom.

This extensive child-proofing was done after the cold, winter evening when I called home from work, prior to teaching a seminar, and was told by my brother, who was there helping my husband, "Everything's fine, just fine, except one thing—we can't find Eric." By that time my husband had been out looking for the last half hour—looking for our one-year-old baby dressed only in pajamas, wandering through a foot of snow on the coldest night of the year! I cried in the toilet stall and prayed, then taught the seminar through my tears and anguish, explaining the situation to my group. An hour later, I got a call. With the help of the police, Eric had been found, three blocks away, shivering in a neighbor's backyard, where he'd once seen a basketball standard. He was just waiting, he said, for someone to come out and "play bathketball!"

I tried not to think of this episode and so many others as I announced to Eric and his five-year-old brother, Collin, who were both downstairs watching television, that I was going to take a nap and would they please play quietly in the basement while I slept. I secured all the bolts, and, smiling, nestled into my first nap in a long time, assuring myself that even if by some miracle Eric were able to get out of the house, he couldn't escape from the backyard. Houdini was contained!

After an hour of blissful rest, I awoke and went downstairs to thank my sons for being so good while I napped. Only Collin was still seated in front of the TV, without a clue or a care as to the whereabouts of two-year-old Eric. I restrained my panic until I'd searched the entire basement and upstairs, sure he had to be somewhere in the house. Then I opened the door from the house to the garage. My mouth flew open as wide as the space of the open garage door as I saw his blanket and realized he'd found the one button to freedom—the garage door opener in my car, taking with him the dog and his favorite green hot-wheels. My heart was pounding as I remembered how high and swift the canals were at this time of year.

Crying Eric's name, I searched the neighborhood on foot and in the car. The neighbors had heard that plaintive cry so many times, they probably just looked out of their windows, shook their heads and said, "It's that poor, psychotic woman again." Shaking, I returned and called the police. Now I had to wait by the phone while they searched. But what mother can wait while her child is in peril? I ran into the backyard, calling his name again and again until I finally fell on my knees in a sobbing prayer. I prayed that fervent mother prayer for my lost child which I had prayed so many times that probably the heavens also were saying, "Look, it's that poor, psychotic woman again." It was that prayer from the depths of my soul where, pleadingly, I promised the Lord that if he would only return my child, I would devote my life to service, and I would cherish with all my heart this dear child he'd given me.

After an agonizing, gruesome hour, a phone call came from the police. They had Eric several blocks away at the elementary school. Apparently, as the students were coming out to recess, a teacher had seen him happily riding his hotwheels on the busy boulevard, the dog running behind him. With some coaxing, she had convinced him to give up his joy ride. I looked to the heavens in heartfelt thanks and raced down to the school, hoping he hadn't slipped past them in a moment of distraction. I ran across the playground, swept that little boy up into my arms and cried, promising myself that I'd never let him out of my sight again.

Of course, it never happened. We were calling the police again the next week. But I came to realize that these heartrending episodes, as painful as they are, can teach and help us. First, the prayers. When do we pray more earnestly than when a child is lost? During those torturous moments, we redevote our lives to that child and to the Lord with promises that, granted, no mortal could ever keep. But it does make us reexamine our lives and realize just how intensely we love that child. I have said many of those prayers. I have made many of those promises.

I prayed those prayers in Disneyland when our eight-year-old ran off after getting in a squabble with his dad about jumping on the handrails. I suppose it was appropriate that he headed for Tomorrowland while his dad, with the other boys, strolled off to Fantasyland with no apparent concern that we'd somehow be reunited. Meanwhile, I wandered through "Woe and Worryland," anxiously calling his name, wringing my hands and wondering if I'd ever see him again. After an hour, he came out of hiding. He'd been darting behind rides and concession stands, watching his worried mother wait.

I prayed those prayers all through the night once when my husband went to the airport in Edinburgh to pick up our son returning from a youth conference in Spain and came home empty-handed. No Adam, and no word as to why. It was the last flight of the day. Unable to reach anyone in Spain by phone, we began wondering if he'd ever made it to the conference. Then we began imagining the nightmarish possibility of his having been abducted in London or left in an alley somewhere. Agonizing hours passed. As I knelt by our fireplace heater that cold night in Scotland, my body weak from fear, I prayed for this boy's well-being from the depths of my soul. How could I have known that he was asleep in the London airport, having forgotten our new phone number and without a thought that we'd be concerned?

In these moments of anguish, I have made such monumental promises that I know if I could ever live up to them, I'd become the first canonized Latter-day Saint! But I've decided that besides moving us to fervent prayer and a more exemplary life (and allowing our children a brief encounter with independence and policemen), the traumatic experience of small children running away helps us prepare for a giant hurdle—the painful moment when our children leave home and we can't go chasing after them.

Sometimes, I can't believe I signed up for a mortal assignment that requires every ounce of my time, energy, and love with one ultimate aim—my obsolescence! Certainly good

mothers do all they can to help their children become independent, responsible, self-sufficient individuals, but once
that's accomplished they put themselves out of a job. I know
the old maxim of "Once a mother, always a mother," but if a
mother has done her work well, her children no longer need
her once they've grown up, at least not in the same way as
when they were in the home. Why would anyone sign up for a
job like that?

One cold winter day, when I was riding up the ski lift
with my five-year-old, he looked down to the hard snow fifty
feet underneath him and said, "If I fell from here, it would be
really sad, wouldn't it?"

With my anxious mother voice, I reassured him, "It would."

"Because I have my whole life to live," he continued. "But
if you fell down, it wouldn't be so sad, 'cause your life's almost
over, isn't it?"

At that moment, I thought maybe it was.

We talk about small children suffering from separation
anxiety when they are removed from their mothers, but what
about the anxiety their mothers experience when their children grow up and begin to separate from them?

When our middle son, Collin, was in eighth grade, we
were arguing over some independence issues one afternoon
as I was driving him to a friend's. At this point, my husband
had died and I was a single parent, struggling to be both the
father and the mother. Finally, I threw up my hands and
said, "Collin, I'm frustrated with all the problems in our relationship!" Without a pause, he put his hand kindly on my
shoulder and, in a mature voice, said, "Mom, I'm sorry, but I
don't think this relationship is going to work. I've decided we
need to start seeing other people." I laughed so hard, I couldn't
remember why I was ever upset. But when the laughter subsided, I heard the unquieting truth—the day was coming
when he really wouldn't need me anymore.

As parents we beg, cajole, and plead for our children to be
more responsible, more independent. "Can't *you* look in the
lost and found *yourself*?" "No, *you* make the call." "How about

finding *yourself* something to eat?" We praise them when they make strides towards independence and berate them when they don't. But when it finally happens, somehow it's not as gratifying as we'd thought.

Recently, I took our oldest son to the airport for a trip to New Zealand with the rugby team. Although I would see him again for a few days when he returned, it felt like a final farewell because we were moving back East and he was going to college at BYU in the fall. He would never really come home again, at least not the coming home that is with friends, after school or football, leaving messages on the board and messes in the kitchen. So this afternoon as I watched the line of black-and-white warm-up jackets waiting for tickets, I was reviewing his life (and mine), asking myself what I'd taught him in almost 18 years and thinking about what I'd forgotten.

Suddenly, it occurred to my mother mind that I should write Adam's name on his jacket, a very smart mother-thing to do, and I was pleased that I'd remembered. It was like one last gesture of my importance in his life. As we walked into the lounge to continue waiting, I noticed a sports bag with the name *Timothy* written in neat letters across the top. I casually asked Adam if there was someone else on the team with his same last name. Complete surprise registered on my face when he told me the bag was his. Struggling to come out of the daze, because in the years I'd known him Adam hadn't written his name on anything (keeping track of things was always my department), I said rather weakly, "That's good, but hand me your jacket and I'll write in *it*." "I already did," was his proud reply. I wonder if he was puzzled by my look of dismay as I feebly remarked, "Oh," because in that one moment I knew that my role of mother, at least mothering as I knew it, was over.

Of course, he's since called from college saying, "What do I do about this parking ticket?" "I missed one of my classes because I couldn't find the building." "How long does this cooked rice last that you sent out with Grandma three weeks ago?" "My soap dish broke." And, "I'm out of money." He still needs me, but it's not the same.

I don't think I'm going to do well in the empty nest. Part of the problem is that I have only three children. For those mothers who have less or none, I remove the word *only* and gratefully, wholeheartedly acknowledge—I have three children. I am so blessed. No complaints. But the truth is, our nest has always seemed a little empty. From the time of childhood, I wanted a "quiver full." So, during the twelve years of infertility procedures, when I used to sit in the ultrasound waiting room with other women who had no children and I had to tell them I already had three, I felt guilty, like I already had more than my share. But when I'm around large families, or even in writing this book with women who have many children, I often look to the heavens and ask, "Why not me?"

For years I felt the Lord was punishing me for some reason. Maybe because I worked part-time; maybe because I wasn't patient enough with the children I had. Maybe he didn't hear my prayers. Maybe he didn't love me.

For years my pattern was two weeks of hope for new life followed by two weeks of grieving the loss. I cried. I pleaded. I tried every type of diet, herb, exercise, naturopath, and specialist. Sometimes I would give up all the medical procedures and rely totally on the Lord. Then I'd go back to the fertility center, thinking maybe the Lord needed a little additional help. I fasted. I prayed. I received blessings. Still no more children. Maybe the Lord thought I wasn't grateful for the ones I had. Didn't he know that it was because of them, because I loved them so much, that I wanted more? Was I wrong to ask?

Although I don't know the answer, I have come to believe that children are not given in a quantity commensurate with the quantity of our righteousness. Our Divine Father gives them as a gift in the number and personalities that He feels will be best for us and for them. But even coming to understand this, I still wish I'd had more children. I still feel the three I've got are too soon leaving the nest. I felt this powerfully last Christmas when, after a madrigal concert at the elementary school, I walked behind my 6-foot-plus son who'd come to perform. Silhouetted in his handsome dark suit, surrounded by his younger cousins and a brother who attended the school, he was making his way down the hall to go see his first-grade teacher. As I followed behind with my mother-in-law, suddenly I burst into tears and cried: "I just walked him down this hall. I just held his hand and showed him the way to that teacher's room. How did he get so tall? When did he grow up and quit needing me?"

But this was the child who was bound for freedom and independence from infancy. He was the one who had escaped from his crib 27 times one night while we were visiting my mom and dad. Finally we pushed the crib into a corner, stood the ping pong table on one end to create a third wall, nailed a tall board to the remaining end, and still considered roofing it in heavy wire mesh. He didn't escape again that night, but ultimately it didn't keep him from leaving home.

And this was the 18-month-old baby who, when I took him Christmas shopping at the mall, escaped three times from his stroller. The first time, he toddled clear to the other end of the mall and listened happily to the Christmas carolers until he was spotted by security, thanks to a family who had been following this baby, wondering where his mother was. The next time he was located running the aisles of another department store, waving a huge black bra that he'd picked up in Ladies' Lingerie. And the last time, he escaped shortly before the stores were closing. I panicked as I chased through stores calling for him. Then I heard a wee cry in the distance. Thank goodness, he had locked himself in one of the dressing rooms!

This was also the same child to whom I offered my help 13 years later when his father was dying of cancer and his independent spirit responded. I asked him if he didn't want to talk and reminded him that, after all, I was a marriage and family therapist and usually people liked to talk to me. Somehow, my qualifications must have fallen short because he looked at me and replied, kindly but sincerely, "Thanks, Mom, but I can talk to my Heavenly Father."

And this is a boy who did. One October evening, when we'd returned home after seeing *Medicine Man,* Adam was determined to sleep outside in a hammock like he'd seen in the movie. I finally consented, but as I was putting on my nightgown, I felt the shivering night air and decided he needed more blankets to keep him from the cold. I grabbed another sleeping bag and headed outside. When I reached the hammock, I stopped. There was Adam with his knees dug in the dirt, kneeling over the hammock, saying his prayers. I was touched and stood silently, pleased, and shaking. It was so cold, I was quite convinced that he wouldn't be long. Three minutes went by, then six, then ten. Then I quit counting. When he finally stood up, I handed him the sleeping bag, and with my quivering voice, more from emotion than from cold, I could only say, "I love you. Sleep well."

I have come to learn that these children are not mine. They belong to their Heavenly Father. I cannot hold on to them, no matter how many bolts I put on the doors. They do not belong to me. They are only loaned to me for a brief period on earth. Sometime they must run. As much as I want to be a central figure in their lives, I want the Savior to be more central in their lives. I need to teach them all I can in our brief but precious time together and then let them go to find their own path. The truth is, children are never running away from home. Through their spirited and sometimes convoluted journey, they are only running one direction, towards home—their heavenly home.

Can I Keep These Plates Spinning?

Ponder this if you've been burned by having
too many irons in the fire

I remember watching the circus on television as a child. In all that excitement, there was one act that absolutely terrified me. It was not the high wire. It was not the trapeze artists. It was the lone man in a black tuxedo who kept 47 china plates spinning simultaneously on top of long, slender poles. I watched this whir of white in awe and horror as the first plate would begin to wobble. (Breaking a plate in our house was nothing less than a tragedy.) But with unwavering focus and the finesse of an Olympic athlete, the circus performer would rescue each plate and re-engage it in its circular hum, and I could begin to breathe again, though not deeply until all the plates were retrieved from this perilous position and stacked securely in his arms!

Through the years, I have come to view motherhood as an overwhelming, circus-plate-spinning experience with hundreds of plates demanding to be spun all at once, each with a voice of urgency which shouts, "Hurry up! You're behind! Catastrophe threatens!" Look out over your own sea of spinning plates. Each child's set of teeth represents a plate. Add more plates for braces. Each head of hair needing cutting or styling denotes a plate. There are plates for changing the baby's diapers, others for emptying the dishwasher, mowing the lawn, helping the kids with homework, and taking out the garbage—all shouting at once to be kept spinning. And let's not forget the myriad plates for driving kids to dance, football, piano, hockey, clarinet, gymnastics, and swimming lessons, not to mention the plate for keeping the batteries to the video camera charged so you can record their games and recitals and, perhaps even more important, the keeping-the-gas-in-the-car plate so you can accomplish the insanity of the above.

Many mothers spin PTA, Scouts, career, and church service plates, along with plates for paying the bills, dealing with insurance companies, matching the socks, returning the library books and videotapes, and remembering the neighbors at Christmas. And what about the mothers who care for handicapped children? That plate alone requires constant and exhaustive spinning. There are heavy—hard-to-keep-spinning—cooking and laundry plates, along with picking-up-the-dry-cleaning, watering-the-plants, keeping-milk-in-the-refrigerator plates, *plus* getting-everybody-to-make-their-beds-and-take-their-vitamins plates. And don't forget the plate for keeping toilet paper in all the bathrooms at all times!

However, even if you are somehow miraculously keeping all these plates spinning, you are inevitably called on to spin the unforeseen crisis plates—mopping up the flood in the basement, taking to the vet the cat who keeps throwing up, repairing a flat tire on your son's bike, calling a repairman to fix your refrigerator (and knocking on your neighbor's door while juggling 50 pounds of frozen goods in your hands and hoping she has room in her freezer), rushing your child, who fell from the treehouse, to the emergency room, preparing dinner for unexpected out-of-town guests, and finding the blue bow with the white trim that your daughter cries she must have or she can't go to school. And disaster can happen the second you turn your back. I had a toddler who, in less than five minutes, could empty four boxes of cereal, all the pasta from their bags, and all the vitamins from the vitamin chest, plus peel six bananas, turn on the stove, and take a stroll across the burners, melting his shoes. My only clue was burning latex!

Mothers have to be perpetual motion machines, always

doing three or more things at once to barely keep up. As a young mother with a new baby, I attended graduate school while supplementing our meager income of student loans by making ceramic Christmas ornaments. (The kiln and molds were bequeathed to me by a former veterinary student's wife so I could make 27 cents an hour like she did and get to stay home with the kids.) I spent innumerable hours hunched over a table, painstakingly painting those ornaments while listening to class lectures I'd taped and at the same time rocking my baby with my feet!

One day, while visiting a friend who is an executive in a very stressful business, my girlfriend (who has six children) and I were listening to him describe his day—a phone in each ear as he is writing a proposal on the computer, signing documents, ten people clamoring at his office door, late for his next meeting, his secretary trying to ask him about flight arrangements, pressed to make critical decisions, and no time to eat (unless it's intravenously). Noticeably unmoved, my puzzled girlfriend and I turned to each other, then looked back at him, and said, sincerely, "So?"

"What do you mean, 'so?'" he questioned, a little disconcerted.

"Our lives are like that every day at home," we continued. "We have to do twenty things at once or we'd never survive. And we don't get to leave the pressure and chaos at the end of the day. It continues through the night and comes bursting in at us again the next day! And, we certainly don't have a personal secretary!"

This was revelation to us as we recognized that our job as mothers was as difficult as—or more difficult than—that of the most stressed of business executives. This understanding was reflected in his final comment. He told us that we'd make good executives. We told him that he'd make a good mother!

In spite of all we do as mothers, all the plates we spin each day, sometimes we feel that we've accomplished nothing. Years ago, I heard a friend's therapist tell her she should occasionally write down just what she did in a day to help her appreciate her multitudinous daily achievements. I have given this assignment to some of my own female clients who were having difficulty feeling validated but I had never used it myself until one Saturday in May. At the end of that day, the list read like this:

—Shower and dress.
—Clean the kitchen from yesterday's rubble.
—Go grocery shopping.
—Unload groceries.
—Cut up oranges, fill thermoses for soccer game.
—Find Eric's baseball uniform.
—Drive Eric to his tournament baseball game.
—Return home and arrange a ride for Collin to get to his soccer game.
—Make French toast for Adam, Collin, and friends Brock and Daniel, who slept over.
—Pick up Eric at his baseball game and drive him to his soccer game with oranges and water.
—Drive Collin to a friend's house who'll take him to soccer.
—Take Brock and Daniel home.
—Drive home to pick up Adam and help him find his cleats.
—Drive Adam to his baseball game.
—Pick up Eric at his soccer game.
—Pick up Collin at his soccer game.
—Take Eric and Collin home.
—Make fast peanut butter sandwiches for lunch.
—Take Eric to his second tournament baseball game.
—Drive to grocery store, get drinks and treats for Adam's baseball game and candy for Matthew's birthday party.
—Drive to toy store to buy present. Store is closed.
—Drive Collin to soccer tryouts.
—Drive to mall to find birthday present.
—Pick up Eric at his baseball game.

—Go to Adam's baseball game (arriving just after he's been up to bat) and drop off drinks and treats.

—Drive back to Eric's baseball field to look for the mitt he's left.

—Pick up Collin and friend at soccer tryouts.

—Take Eric, Collin, and a friend to 7–11 for slurpees, then home.

—Drive Eric to Matthew's birthday party.

—Return to Adam's baseball game to pick him up and find the field empty.

—Return home, get phone call from Collin to deliver his swimsuit at a friend's house.

—Drop off swimsuit.

—Go pick up my friend.

—Drive across town to set up tables at a fund-raiser for a political campaign.

—Set up tables, listen to a speech, eat two chocolate-covered strawberries, take my friend home.

—Pick up Eric from the birthday party.

—Pick up Collin from his friend's.

—Make several calls to find Adam. Ask him to please walk home. Tell him whatever's in the fridge from dinner three nights ago is his.

—Fall into bed.

Although that list was not particularly awe-inspiring reading, it helped me to see how many plates I kept spinning in a day. Reviewing it, I realized that much of my insanity could be eliminated if (1) the verb *drive* didn't exist, and (2) I didn't allow my boys to play sports, have friends, or eat. However, I happen to believe that all these things are important in the development of children—essential plates worth spinning. And so, like many other mothers, I've learned how to be a perpetual motion machine; however, in the process I've had to let some plates slow down, others fall and break. For example (or as a confession), I drive my kids to school in my nightgown (with a prayer that I won't run out of gas). I don't

wear makeup. I own only one pair of earrings, so I never have
to spend time deciding which ones to wear. I don't make my
bed unless we're having an open house. I cook the same meal
every Sunday. I eat leftovers cold, out of the pan, to save
washing another dish. My plate for ironing fell 18 years ago
after, as a young bride, I spent three and a half hours ironing
my husband's 27 shirts. I soon mastered the art of spray and
smooth—a little water from the spray bottle, a little smooth
of the hand. It's not perfect, and it's a disgrace for someone
whose mother won the ironing division of the Mrs. Utah con-
test in 1957, but it works!

The truth is, through the years, a number of my plates
have shattered. Many are wobbling. And the voice behind
them has changed. This didn't happen just because I couldn't
keep up anymore. Although I couldn't. (Sometimes I think it
might have begun 20 years ago when, attending a church
homemaking meeting, I was given a handout entitled "Washing Windows Can Be Painless," with a recipe for "homemade
Windex" and a suggestion to "wipe all the windows with glyc-
erine every two or three days to keep them from steaming."
What if I had taken that lesson seriously? I'd have become a
crazed woman, consumed with making my own Windex and
washing my windows every other day. I've kept that handout
for those moments when I need to laugh, hysterically!)

Actually, it was a change in perspective that altered my
plate spinning and made me view everything I did as a
mother differently. Perhaps it began when I first read the
near-death experience in George Ritchie's book, *Return from
Tomorrow*, in which the glorious being of light asks him what
he has done with his life. After reviewing his worldly accomplishments—such as having become an Eagle Scout and having been accepted into medical school—he realizes to his horror and amazement that the only question he's being asked,
the only question he'll ever really be asked is "How much
have you *loved* with your life?"

Now, I know this is probably not a new thought for you,
and it was not a new thought for me. But when I read it, it

hit me as though I were hearing it for the first time, and I cried inside, "How much *have* I loved with my life?" Suddenly my long list of daily demands, my endless plate spinning, seemed only important in accomplishing this one goal, and I began a new way of looking at my role as a mother. I also had a friend whose constant advice through my continual struggle was, "Remember, we are only here to love." When this was the banner over all my tasks, my frantic spinning plates were changed into opportunities to love. Now I had only one main plate to spin, and the voice behind it was asking how much I was loving. It gave new meaning to the lilies of the field who "toil not, neither do they spin"! (Matthew 6:28.)

I still had many things to accomplish in a day, but seeing what needed to be done through changed eyes gave me more patience and more delight in life. I began to realize that each spin of the plate is either a chance to love or just a chance to spin another plate. I began appreciating my children's sense of time and need for exploration instead of seeing them as threats to completing the next task on my list. I realized that children don't indulge in plate spinning; if they do, it's only one plate at a time because they live wholly in the present, immersing themselves in whatever they're doing.

As a young mother, before I understood we are only here to love, I felt great conflict in me and in our home. For example, while I was spinning my myriad plates with an emphasis on the plate called "let's get through dinner, *now!*" my son was in the bathroom seeing how many bubbles he could make in the sink and then pile in a pyramid on his arm, instead of just washing his hands and coming to dinner. When after much prodding he finally made it to dinner, he built a mashed potato fort, landscaped with broccoli trees and rows of peas for ammunition, instead of just eating. We were obviously focused on very different plates—and in very different ways.

Only eyes that are looking to love can begin to see such moments with wondrous appreciation instead of as frustrating inconveniences in our daily schedules. As often as we practice the words, children are seldom motivated by "Hurry up! Do more! You're behind." Their internal system defies this command and says instead "Slow down; observe; experience; put your hands, feet, and mouth on it; love it, whatever it is!" If we watch closely, they will teach us how to come back to this centered, joyous place.

Our youngest son at age five was such a naturally good swimmer that he qualified to compete with his team at the regional swim meet championship. I was there at the side of the pool, like the 6:00 news team, my huge video camera perched on my shoulder, ready to capture the race of this incredible backstroker. At the sound of the gun, all the swimmers took off as though they were being shot from cannons, all except Eric, who began his leisurely swim, delighted to be on his back so he could see all the dragons and clowns and castles in the afternoon clouds above him.

As the other swimmers touched the finish, all eyes went to the last boy, who was slowly and happily zigzagging his way through the water, and to his mother, who was painfully filming each stroke and encouraging him in vain to hurry up since the entire meet was waiting on him. After several grueling minutes, he finally reached the other side, climbed out of the pool, and beaming with the look of a champion exclaimed, "I did *good*, didn't I!" What could I say? He had! Much better than his mother, who had thought the point of the race was to swim the fastest and thus win. This little boy *had* won!

One evening, four years later, while we were living in Scotland, we were waiting for this same son to return from the beach so we could leave for a family dinner appointment. As the light faded, our anger grew. We were furious at this inconsiderate child for making us all late. His older brother had left the beach on time, encouraging him to come. But with Eric, there were always a few more sea urchins to find, a few more tide pools to explore.

Finally, in great fury, we drove down to the shore and found this selfish child at work in the sand. As we began ranting, tears sprang to his eyes, and he pointed to the spot on which we were standing—an enormous heart drawn in the sand and filled in with hundreds of carefully hand-picked sea shells. Crying, he told us that it was the grave marker for a dead bird he'd found on the beach, which he felt needed a proper burial. When asked why it had to be so large, he sobbed, "It was a very big bird!"

We have a friend, Fay Schreyer, whose oldest son was born with a strong body and a handicapped mind. As a teenager, Steven's physical prowess enabled him to enter the Special Olympics as the projected winner in track. He was fast. On the day of the race, he took off like lightning and was many yards ahead of his competitors when suddenly he realized he was alone—his friends were not with him. He stopped, turned around, and, seeing them in the distance, grinned and ran back to greet them and help all of them complete the race together. As he finally came across the finish line, making sure the others crossed to victory before him, a whisper spread through the stunned audience acknowledging that he could have easily won the gold medal. Instead he won whatever is a million steps above gold. We are the ones who are handicapped—at least spiritually and morally. We think life is about finishing the race first. Our children teach us that the winner is the one who finishes the race with the most love and compassion, the one who enjoys the journey and focuses first on helping others get across the finish line.

So, do I always remember to see each moment, each spinning plate only as an opportunity to love? No, I forget. I forget all the time. I still get caught up in the tasks of life, but then, inevitably, one of my children brings me back to what matters. In their wonderful, inventive, and innocent way, they remind me again why I'm here and help me look through eyes of love.

One evening while I was standing at the sink, which was so piled with dishes I wasn't sure there was a sink, except for the sound of running water underneath—stringy hair in my face; an old, food-stained apron hanging over my shoulders; feeling overburdened, overwhelmed, overweight, and unloved—my three-year-old, who had been sent to bed five times already, peeked into the kitchen, wearing his Superman cape and Burger King crown. Before I could scold him one more time to get back to bed, he exclaimed, "Mommy, Mommy, I da pwince, and you da . . . you da . . ."

"I the what?" I responded, still a little exasperated, but softening at this child's tender petition.

"I da pwince," he continued, "and you da, oh, what's da girl?"

"The girl?" I asked. "You mean the princess?"

"Yeah!" he shouted joyously, then looked up at me with bright, twinkling eyes and said, "I da pwince an' you da pwincess, and let's dance!"

As I picked up my little boy and we waltzed through the kitchen that evening, I didn't look back at the plates in the sink or the plates in my life. In that moment, I was the princess, and I was dancing with the prince. In that moment, I saw only love.

Full Circle

Healing balm for those who have lost
a loved one to a terminal illness

As I gazed at the frail, agonized body of my husband, oozing with bed sores, my heart felt anguish to see this once-strong frame now so deteriorated after his almost eight-year fight with brain cancer. My dear neighbor and nurse friend, looking at that same tattered body, commented lovingly and almost brightly, "Look at how nicely he's progressing!" When Steve's mother and I exchanged a puzzled glance, my neighbor clarified in that soothing, wise voice, "What I mean is, look at how, as his body grows weaker, his spirit grows so much stronger." It was true. He was progressing.

Steve, who had once been a robust member of the University of Colorado ski team, with muscular prowess that enabled him to fly up the foothills of the Flatiron mountains ahead of the pack, was now an almost silent shell, having no way to communicate with us except for the tears that still ran down his face when something very tender touched him. But here was a man who, having once fought the adult struggles of pride and anger and depression, had become what we all need to become before we leave this earth—a little child, "willing to submit to all things which the Lord seeth fit to inflict upon [us]" (Mosiah 3:19). Becoming as a little child is the ultimate progression.

When my husband and I were first married and living in our tiny three-room apartment, we began the occasional ritual of taking a walk around the block at night to discuss our goals and life's most pressing problems. My husband's began with "If only I can get into veterinary school" and progressed to "If only I can get *out* of veterinary school!" My cry, "If only I can get pregnant," soon became "If only I can get this baby through his first year!"

Initially we believed that enough laps around the block would allow us to achieve our goals and arrive at some bliss-ful, problem-free state—with us in control of our lives. But no matter how many times we circled, no matter how many laps we made around that block, we never achieved all our goals, and there was always an endless stream of problems. It seemed we prayed for blessings and received more trials. But what we didn't know, what we couldn't have known then, is that often the trial *is* the blessing and that it wasn't as much a matter of solving as it was a matter of submitting—submit-ting to the Lord's will, something our strong-willed, adult spirits fight to the finish as we instead look to the heavens and shout, "Why are you picking on me!"

When I received the phone call that December afternoon saying that my husband had been taken to the University Medical Center after experiencing a grand mal seizure, my heart sank into my stomach and fear filled its place in my chest. I did not want this trial! Quickly, I gathered my three small sons; holding hands, we knelt in a circle and offered a tearful prayer that the Lord would help us, that he'd make things right and put our lives back together the way we had known them. But life was never to be the same again. It was to be harder. It was to be better.

I believe the Lord looks at most of our trials as potential progression, as a means of humbling us so we can become as little children. I don't think he laughs when we look up at him and cry that the ensuing trial is too hard, but he proba-bly smiles like a coach who's just asked us to run the steps of an entire stadium and, putting his hand supportingly on our back, says, "This will be good for you!"

After hours of interminable waiting, the neurosurgeon walked slowly into the room, shook his head, took off his mask, and said solemnly, "It looks much worse than I had expected. I'm sorry." Steve's mother and I stood paralyzed, then stumbled our way down a long corridor until we found sanctuary in a room of exercise equipment; here in this room that symbolizes challenge and hard work, we dropped to our knees and let our tears fall over an old bench press as we pleaded with the Lord to save Steve and to let him raise his children. "Save" is exactly what the Lord had in mind, but not the way we defined it.

When the day finally arrived to bring Steve home from the hospital, we streamed into his room with balloons and happy faces that tried not to look too surprised at the changed appearance of this man who'd once had a thick head of dark hair. But my three-year-old, his eyes fixed on my husband's head, quickly blurted out, "Where's yo hair?"

"It's gone," my husband replied with a smile.

"Can the docto put back yo hair?"

"No, son."

This little boy paused for a moment, then climbed up on his father's lap, rubbed his hand vigorously across his dad's bristly, stitched scalp, and exclaimed, "Dat's okay. I like pwickely hair!"

Little children have a way of looking at the world with such acceptance that they submit naturally to the will of the Lord. If only we trusted his plan for us this much.

Initially we were consumed with the fight against cancer—making fresh carrot juice each morning, researching all the recent literature on brain tumors (I threw it all away when I read the prognosis was only two years), cooking macrobiotic meals with the right seaweed, and helping Steve learn creative visualization to reduce the size of the tumor. Skiing took on new meaning as he visualized himself taking several runs down the tumor to shave off a little of the malignant growth each day. Now our walks around the block were

focused on ways to fight cancer, to fight death, the only victory in our eyes being life. Life was exactly what the Lord
had in mind for Steve, but not as we understood it.

In time, the effusive concern subsided, and Steve's illness
became part of day-to-day living. Taking him for radiation
treatments was put on the list along with grocery shopping
and taking kids to the dentist. Some days it was hard juggling children and a husband who was not well. I remember
a number of times running from stirring a pot of soup for dinner to helping Steve through another grand mal seizure
while simultaneously being loudly summoned by a child to
come back and help him with his math homework! One
morning when I was rushing to get Steve to the hospital, our
youngest son, refusing to go to school, barricaded his bedroom door with every piece of furniture in his bedroom. It
was like the stand at the Alamo. Banging on the door was of
no use. I could have called the fire department, but wouldn't
they have wondered why the parents had fled? And even if
they could have unearthed this child from his bedroom,
would they have known which shirt he wanted to wear and
remembered to put his lunch money in his backpack? Needless to say, he won.

But the ingeniousness of children, and why I think we
must become like them, is that they don't come to a paralyzing halt in the face of adversity. They don't wither, go to bed,
and give up. They may not handle it all correctly in our eyes,
but their life force, their creative momentum, is so strong
that they take the objectionable, turn it around and upside
down, and figure out a way to keep going (and often with
some measure of mirth). They submit without surrendering.

Our boys approached the solemnity of the hospital setting
with intrigue and irreverence. When the nurse was out of the
room, they jacked up the hospital beds into their most contorted positions; made "bombs" out of the tongue depressors
(something their mother had taught them to do by weaving
Popsicle sticks together); blew up the surgical gloves, drew
funny faces on them, and popped them, if they were really

brave. One of our most exciting visits to the hospital was when our three-year-old pulled the fire alarm. Prior to this, I didn't know what happens when a fire alarm goes off in a hospital. I learned quickly. Everyone scrambled in great commotion, and three shiny fire engines, each a city block long, pulled up in front of the hospital, sirens blaring. My son witnessed all of this as, en masse, we were sheepishly exiting, trying hard to look like the rest of the crowd and not like the perpetrators of such panic. His only comment was: "Fun! Let's do it again!"

They see it all so differently. One day, we were in the middle of an "X-Men" birthday party, the house swelling with nine-year-olds, each dressed in the most garish and grotesque X-Men costumes they could find, when Steve wandered out of the bedroom, looking rather pale and cadaverous, with purple rings under his eyes and a blood-filled tube draining from his scalp. There was a short pause as the adults looked uneasy, then suddenly one of the boys exclaimed sincerely, "Eric, your dad's got the best costume of all. But which X-Man *is* he?"

Steve went through endless rounds of nauseating, experimental chemotherapy, more radiation, and another brain surgery in his fight to live. But more than just wanting to live, he wanted life, and he began appreciating life through more childlike eyes. He now wept at the sight of a beautiful sunrise, began riding his bike to work, and announced on the day he watched his cherished BMW being towed for illegal parking that he "forgave the policeman on the spot!" Time became precious. He didn't know how little or how much he had of it, he only knew each moment was a gift. When I complained one birthday about getting older, he exploded justifiably with, "I want as many birthdays as I can have!"

He decided we should take a year-long sabbatical, traveling through Europe and living in Scotland. When we announced our plans to the neuro-oncologist, he said it was impossible. We strengthened our resolve, and he finally suggested a massive dose of radiation just prior to departure. I believe it was the joy of being in Europe as a family more than the radiation that sustained Steve, but whatever it was, he darted through the cities of Europe with such incredible energy that when the rest of us would finally catch up and scold him for leaving us behind, he'd just smile and say, "Keep your eye on the red cap!" We did, as the faithful among the children of Israel did with the serpent. But what a horrible moment when one of the children realized they were following a red cap without their dad underneath it!

When the rains of Scotland became cold and Steve's seizures returned full force, we ended our sojourn—only a couple of weeks ahead of schedule—and returned home to get Steve some help. To us it was just another round to fight, at least that's what we kept telling ourselves. But when the neurosurgeon brought out the MRI scans, we must have been holding our breath because we both gasped. The tumor had almost tripled in size since the scan taken in Edinburgh only weeks previously. And those dark, fingerlike projections had now crossed into the other hemisphere. "I wouldn't recommend surgery," said the neurosurgeon in his kind but dry tone. "At best it would only give you a few extra months and would most likely leave you entirely paralyzed on the left side of your body."

We left there stunned. In seven years we'd never faced a prognosis so grim. Death had never seemed imminent, but now we had it in black and white. Still, we had to believe we could beat it, even though daily Steve was becoming worse. One morning, I left him sleeping to go to our oldest son's basketball game, a feeble attempt at being a supportive mother. Our youngest, Eric, was still celebrating his birthday party sleepover, which he'd organized entirely on his own. I'd hardly remembered it was his birthday. As I walked into the kitchen, I did remember the spectacular theme birthdays we'd planned together, like the pirate party where we built our own pirate ship, discovered a treasure chest, walked the plank for prizes, and had a piñata. I'd used my utmost culinary skills to make a chocolate treasure chest cake full of gold coins. This morning I wasn't even sure I'd said hello to the group of boys our son had gathered from the night before. I decided the theme of this party was "You're on your own." I told them I'd be gone an hour. I don't think they looked up.

While I was at Adam's game, the pressure on Steve's brain became so great that he began experiencing violent seizures and projectile vomiting. Eric did his nine-year-old best to help him, but he finally called Steve's mom to come to the rescue. When I got home, we loaded Steve in the car and headed for the emergency room. He spent two days in intensive care. He stabilized, but we knew he needed more help. Finally, we opted for the risk of surgery at M. D. Anderson, a marvelous cancer hospital in Houston, and Steve began thinking about options like teaching high school biology from a wheelchair, if in fact he became paralyzed. We were hopeful, and everyone fed that hope, from the surgeons to the little British lady in an apron who first greeted us, to the men sweeping the floors from whom we asked directions.

Again, I waited with Steve's mother during those grueling hours of surgery. I remember the cold tile in the bathroom cubicle where I fell to my knees many times that day, and I remember the faces of others who, like us, waited and agonized. We prayed for them too. And they prayed for us. The boys could not be with us, but they wanted to fast. On the day of surgery, our middle son sat down in the school cafeteria without a lunch and was asked why he wasn't eating. When he told his friends he was fasting for his father, they pushed their lunches aside and said, "Then we'll fast too!"

Those prayers were heard. The surgeon fairly bounced into the waiting room and announced that 70 to 90 percent of the tumor had been removed, releasing the tremendous pressure on Steve's brain—and with no apparent paralysis. We were ecstatic, and so grateful. Hope flowed into our family as we brought Steve home—walking, happy, planning his future.

For a few weeks he seemed to prosper, then he progressed from faltering steps to a walker and finally to a wheelchair. Impressed in my mind is one particular Sunday morning when Steve's dad came and helped that frail body from the bed to the wheelchair and into the shower. I felt such sweet tears as I saw him kneeling and tenderly washing Steve's feet, as the water poured over them, especially poignant since it was Father's Day.

As Steve's care required more attention than family could render, someone suggested we use the services of hospice in our home. I wouldn't consider it. Hospice was for people who are dying. Steve wasn't dying. At least that's what I kept telling myself. He was getting better.

He *was* getting better. Daily he was becoming more guile-less and childlike, more grateful for everything we did for him. In the middle of the night when his urinary catheter would come undone and the bed would be soaked, I'd get him up, clean him, and tuck him back into fresh sheets. He'd look up at me with the eyes of a child and say, "Thanks for taking care of me."

I wish I could say I was that patient and supportive every second of his illness, but there were a few times that I went into overload. Prior to one surgery to install a dual "port" in Steve's chest to receive direct infusion chemotherapy, I was sorting through bills on the waiting room floor. We had just returned from Scotland, and there was considerable debt and a mountain of paperwork to address. Suddenly, my sorting uncovered a bill for a credit card Steve had told me nothing about, demanding several thousand dollars.

I was too upset to be tactful. When he had no decent ex-planation, I blurted out: "I'm going to kill you! Don't worry about dying from this surgery, because I'm going to kill you right now!" All the eyes in the waiting room turned to stare at the caustic, hysterical woman who had so little regard for the infirm. Ashamed, I followed Steve into the pre-op area where the nurse gave him a surgical gown and asked for his wedding ring which, through countless surgeries and proce-dures, I'd always held safely. This time he told the nurse he didn't want me there and *not* to give me his ring! With my head hung to conceal my tears, I returned to gather my bills from the waiting room. I think everyone there looked away.

I must admit there were times when I felt like Steve was becoming more exalted while I was only becoming more exhausted. Caring for a spouse with a terminal disease can be overwhelming. But, in truth, I did not begin to bear it alone: "Yea, the Lord did strengthen them that they could bear up their burdens with ease, and they did submit cheerfully and with patience to all the will of the Lord" (Mosiah 24:15). As I watched Steve submit humbly to the will of the Lord, it allowed me to do the same. In reflection, this was one of the sweetest times in our lives. In truth, it was not difficult to care for someone who showed such childlike gratitude and grace. I had lived with Steve through earlier years when the darkness of depression had threatened to consume him. Perhaps it was a then-undetected tumor that pulled him into that despair; if so, that same tumor was now launching him into the light of hope. I had been in the battle against spiritual death. Fighting physical death was sweet in comparison.

As Steve's physical capacity decreased, he became increasingly "meek, humble, patient, and full of love" (Mosiah 3:19). There was honestly never a word of complaint, never a word of frustration. Instead, he humbly endured. If we became busy talking while he was struggling to feed himself—which sometimes meant five minutes in an arduous effort to get one bite on his fork (which usually held nothing by the time it reached his mouth)—he would patiently try again without a word. If we dropped him while trying to help him walk or forgot to give him his medications or empty his urine bag or a dozen other nursing skills we fumbled at, he waited quietly. One day, when he was naked, frail, left alone in the bathroom for his privacy, Steve's mom got worried after he'd been there quite awhile and still hadn't blown his whistle to say he was done. In an anxious voice, she called in and asked, "Are you okay?" After a moment's thought, a kind, small voice—from a body that had slipped to the cold tile floor, wedged upside down between the wall and the toilet—answered back positively, "Well, kind of!"

I don't know when I crossed over the line between holding

on and letting go. Submitting to Steve's illness was one thing. Submitting to his death was another. I think it must have come gradually in moments of understanding. One day, while taking apart the disposal—which hadn't worked for two weeks—I was crying to my mother-in-law, "What will I do when he's gone? Who will take care of these things?" Before my tears reached the ground, I stopped, looked up, and said, "What am I talking about? The one who will take care of these things is the one who has always taken care of these things—me!" It was true that the one time Steve had determined to help around the house, he had stood on the kitchen table to change a light bulb and the whole table had flipped over, nearly killing him and splitting the stand into pieces. I began to laugh through my tears as I realized that the Lord had been preparing me for this for years. I had been married to a veterinarian who was never home. Not only could I repair the disposal, I could lay sod, deal with the insurance companies, and attend boys' maturation night with all the fathers. I could do all that, but I still didn't want to be alone.

One afternoon as we sat by the creek, he said tearfully, "I do not want to leave you and the children, but . . ." His voice choked as he began to sob, "I *do* want to go home." As I gradually accepted his journey home, I began to see how the process of death mirrors the process of birth and allows us to come full circle. Instead of treasuring his first word, we treasured his last. Instead of happily anticipating his first breath, we anxiously awaited his last. With birth, the spirit must find a way to enter the tiny, newly forming body, but with death, the spirit must find its way out of that body, and sometimes it's difficult.

When Steve's breathing became labored, we were told he had very little time left. But he would not give in, perhaps because he felt our unwillingness to let him go. One afternoon, Steve's dear mission president, Robert V. Stevens, came with his wife. In giving Steve a blessing, he instructed him to use his priesthood to help his spirit be released from his body. He then said, "Your work in this life is over. The

Lord is pleased with you, and your Heavenly Father waits for you with open arms. You have a glorious mission awaiting you." Those words were joyous to us. They changed the way we looked at his parting. They allowed us to finally let go. How appropriate that his mission president should be the one to tell him of his next call. Steve *was* progressing.

When the attending nurses told us that Steve couldn't possibly live through the night, we gathered the boys.

After the family good-bye, I let each of the boys have time alone with their dad. Earlier in the illness, when he was still able to speak, they had come to him with a good report card, a play-by-play of the soccer game, or a bird with a broken wing, but as he became less communicative, it was awkward for them. Still, it seemed important for each to have a moment alone to say good-bye. I noticed later that night how each of them dealt with grief in their own style. Adam played surging music on the piano, Eric drew pictures of war creatures, and Collin went outside and lit firecrackers!

Several nights followed in which we were told Steve could not live through another. I tried to keep myself at constant vigilance, but the moment he chose to die I was in the kitchen on the phone, stirring the dinner and trying to make arrangements for someone who could speak Spanish to attend the back-to-school night with our exchange student. His mother heard his last breath. I came in at her call, and we both sat and marveled at the light in the room but no longer in his body. He was on his way home, as a little child, to the loving arms of his Father. He had progressed.

As the house began to fill with the tears and the tender conversation of family and friends, each of the boys came home from soccer and football practice. I wondered how they would respond, walking into that room. Submitting, like children, each of them acknowledged that it had to be. Adam said he was just happy that his dad was finally free. Collin cried the most. And I knew Eric understood when I saw him put his arm around his cousin who was sobbing and say: "Don't cry, Daniel. My dad isn't dead. He's just gone on to another mission."

Earlene Blaser

Earlene was born and raised in Providence, Utah (Cache Valley). Her childhood was very happy and secure. She felt very important because everyone in town knew who she was. She was named after her dad, Earl Anderson, who was the bishop and a city councilor. Her mom, Emma, worked hard in all the Church and civic organizations, and won blue ribbons at every county fair.

Because Earlene wanted to "go away" to college, she moved to the dorms seven miles away and attended Utah State University. She was a senior when she met her future husband, Steve Blaser, who had just finished an MBA and CPA. She was engaged in six weeks and married in another six (she does not advise this for *anyone!*). After eleven years and pregnant with their sixth child, she finally graduated from USU in 1981. Her husband is the founder of a successful family business.

Earlene has eight children, including Brady, who was born with a rare form of muscular dystrophy and is on a ventilator at home. She has been a room mother zillions of times (at least it seems to feel that way) and high school PTA president. She organized the award-winning Woods Cross marching band rifle corps and choreographed several high school musicals. In 1986 she was chosen Utah Young Mother of the Year (the children say that was the year before the award judges "found her out"). She has served in Church callings at both ward and stake levels.

I Can't Even Imagine

For mothers who have experienced a stress
fracture from carrying heavy burdens

People often ask, "What is it like to have a handicapped child?" Each time I wonder, "Do they *really* want to know?" How do you explain an entire lifestyle in a few sentences? So I answer truthfully, "It's a great learning experience." But like most problems in life (which everyone has), we can't really understand them until we live them ourselves.

Recently a former nurse of Brady's called me from the hospital and asked if I could talk to the mother of a new quadriplegic. He was a thirteen-year-old involved in an automobile accident. He was going to be on a respirator for the rest of his life, and she said his mother wasn't handling it well. This nurse thought that I could be the most help to her, that I had had no problem coping with Brady. I should be flattered. I wasn't. I just felt inadequate. How do I be honest and not negative, realistic and not overwhelming? It's like telling a young bride what marriage is really like or a new mom that her days of sleep are over; I don't think that she will believe me.

How do I tell this mom that her life will never be "normal," that she will never have a day without worry? Her insurance, if she has any, will at best cover 80 percent of the bills. At worst, they will cancel her. If her husband is self-employed, the family will become uninsurable; if not, he will be "job-locked"—he can never change employment because he will lose his insurance. If her child is under 18 years old, they will have no relief from medical bills unless they go on welfare. The home she lives in will have to be extensively remodeled or the family will have to move. She will spend many, many hours every week keeping records of bills and medications. Doctor appointments will eat up several more hundreds of hours. She will become an advocate even if her personality isn't aggressive.

Do I tell her that the divorce rate for parents of handicapped children is significantly higher than the average? Even with the most supportive husband, the main care and responsibility of her son will fall on her shoulders. Do I tell her now that her family will never go swimming or hiking or camping together again? Travel is next to impossible. Commercial airlines are out. If she has help from family, neighbors, and friends, which she will need, she will lose all sense of privacy.

The problem doesn't go away—ever. We don't have periods of stress and then some relief. We have stress every day. The only reprieve would be death. Great alternative?

This mother will learn about new occupations like *physiatrist* and *pulmonologist*. She will feel like she has been to medical school after she learns to interpret medical jargon. She will have to know how to work with the education system and spend time in meetings like IEPs (individual education plans). She most likely will be told that she is doing too much or not enough for her son, sometimes in the same day. Her self-image will have to be restructured quickly, and she will have to guard against being a martyr and using her title of Mother of the Handicapped as her sole identity—or as a crutch. She will have to give up her independence: it will take two people to simply shower her son. Normal things like dressing may take hours, and routine grooming like shaving and brushing teeth will be difficult. Haircuts of bedridden patients are even more challenging. After she figures all of that out, this mother must then educate her bishop, pastor, or priest how to include her son in religious services. Access to public buildings of all kinds has improved much, but there were many church buildings that Brady couldn't even enter *if* we could find parking that would allow wheelchair access. I had one friend whose handicapped daughter never had any-one else but her for a Primary or Sunday School teacher. Year after year, the bishop called the mother to be her teacher, fig-uring that she knew her child best.

Several years ago the University of Michigan Graduate Department of Counseling sent out surveys about ventilator dependent children living at home. (In previous years, chil-dren had been permanently hospitalized.) My son Brady was one of the first patients in Utah to live at home on a ventila-tor. These forms were to be filled out by fathers, mothers, and siblings over twelve years old. Without consulting each other, the participants in the survey were to mail their responses back in separate envelopes and remain anonymous. Several months later the survey was published nationally, addressed to counseling and social work professionals. Copies were also sent to the families who participated. The results showed overwhelming support for the benefits of these children being cared for at home. Their physical and mental health was vastly improved. The siblings coped better with the child at home, and fathers were more involved and satisfied with the arrangements. The moms—*surprise!*—were prone to more illness, anxiety attacks, feelings of alienation, and depres-sion. Would this mom understand when I told her that she would crave sleep like some people crave chocolate, or drugs?

I didn't even want to talk to this mom. It sounded over-whelming, and just thinking about it made me anxious. What good could I possibly do at this point?

How could I possibly, after telling her all these things, ex-plain that I wouldn't trade any of it? That may almost seem cruel. I wish Brady didn't have to suffer or be in any pain, but the experience is undeniably the best my family has had. My children don't know a stranger. They adapt to change and disappointments readily. They are unselfish and know how to share. Things are not as important as people. The children have all repeatedly seen the power of the priesthood in action. My husband is more patient and accepting than he was by nature. My family have been firsthand recipients and witnesses to charitable deeds done for them. They have learned to serve and how to be served. It is the greatest opportunity I can imagine to help my children begin to feel the way God feels, to see things as he would. Having Brady in our home is like living with a saint. His goodness and spirit penetrate all of our lives. If any brother or sister has to do an essay or answer a question about who is a hero in their lives, they always center their answer on Brady. He sustains homesick missionary brothers in the field with a desire to live up to their potential. Every day I tell him that I'm going to turn him over to see if he has wings because he is an angel in my life.

I would tell this mom that she is in for a life-changing experience for good. She will know things that others don't. She will see kindness in people that maybe wasn't even there before. She will feel an unspoken instant bond with other mothers who have trials. I know, love, and appreciate the many mothers whom I haven't yet met in person but who have "been there." Her extended family may love her more and she will gain a greater capacity for accepting herself, her family, and others.

It isn't the hardest thing in the world. She will learn to live each day one at a time. Life's problems come along at different stages, but everyone will have huge obstacles to overcome sometime in their life. You often hear the saying that if everyone put their problems in a pile and you got to choose your life's trials, you would choose the same ones you cast in the pile. It is true for me. I wouldn't trade anyone. Living with Brady has taught me commitment. My children are not afraid of the unknown; they seek friendship with people who are different from themselves. My oldest daughter studied American Sign Language at BYU so she could be supportive of her new friends. As a small child, she always wished that someday she would have a Down Syndrome baby; when one of her girlfriends did, my daughter felt that her friend was lucky. All the children, when old enough, were counselors at muscular dystrophy camp. They got their friends involved, and they love it. My oldest two children's spouses said that the way my children treated Brady was a big attraction to them. They knew what kind of fathers and mothers my children would be.

Brady never leaves my mind. I looked at him this morning as he rang his buzzer at 6:10 A.M. and thought, *He can't do anything for himself.* This time he needed the urinal, but the summons might have been to scratch his nose, put pillows under his legs, or just to reassure him that I was there. He can't even turn his head by himself. He is already legally blind with rapidly decreasing eyesight. He cannot chew food and is fed through a tube directly inserted in his stomach. He appears to have nothing. In reality, he has everything. He has a family who adores him. He has two nieces that he worships. He has friends I haven't even met. He has influenced more people for good than either of us will ever know. Nearly everything that is of an eternal nature is his, especially relationships. He has a best friend that he sees every day. He loves his high school principal like an older brother; he has aunts and an uncle who visit him weekly. He gives and receives unconditional love. He is remembered in prayers literally around the world. He is patient and forgiving. He is smart and wise. He is endearing and kind.

Brady is everything that any mother would want her son to be. He knows his Heavenly Father loves him. I do too. He knows God is real. So do I. How can I express enough thanks for Brady in my life?

She's in for a treat. Would she ever understand that?

I Don't See You Listening

Learning how to exercise your physical ears
with teenagers and spiritual ears with the Lord
can save your relationships or even your life

A good listener is a premium in any organization or relationship and possesses a skill that can truly be considered a gift. For most of us, however, listening is an acquired skill. It does not come easy for many people, especially a natural gabber like myself. My own mother used to hurt my feelings when she would beg me to "just give my ears a rest." Twenty years later, I understand. I was always in trouble in school and church for talking so much and was labeled as being too "social." I had to learn the lost art of listening.

If anyone ever asks what year I was chosen as Utah Young Mother of the Year, the kids will tell them it was "the year before they found her out." "Mother, you're not listening," was only one of their many accusations about my lack of parenting skills. It didn't take me long into motherhood to realize that children think you listen with your eyes, not with your ears. If both eyes are not focused directly on them, they will take your head and twist it as if you were some Houdini-like contortionist, just to make sure that you are listening. (I have tried to explain to them that this is a dangerous move when I am driving.) Instead, I have found it both safer and more effective to kneel down to my child's eye level, take his chin in my hand, and focus on his face. I think this has paid off because now my fourteen-year-old stoops down to listen to me. Occasionally not taking this approach has kept my neck very limber.

Despite the success of making both ear and eye contact, I have discovered that it is best to listen with my heart. "Bite your tongue," a counselor friend suggested as she was asked for tips on raising adolescents. She claimed that her lips were almost always bloody when she had four teenagers at once. Sometimes just piercing your lips shut tight until the other person finishes is the only way not to jump in with what you know is the truth—the right and only way.

One night my oldest was late coming home. He had gone out with his best friend and some girls whom they had met at the mall (can you imagine?). I hadn't a clue who the girls were or where the group had gone. I admit I had been spoiled because I had the luxury of knowing most of my children's friends. It wasn't a family rule or anything, I just enjoyed being with them. The hour was late enough that I had progressed straight through *mad* and was now at *worry*. I planned to let him have it with both guns when he got home. I had visions of him in sackcloth and ashes repenting while he endured his sentencing of being grounded for the rest of his teenage life. I vacillated between feeling scared and angry numerous times. All mothers of teenagers know exactly what I mean: after you see they are alive, you give a war whoop and tell the world that you are going to "kill 'em." The prayer that started in my heart turned full bloom on my knees as I pleaded that he was safe and that I would see him again. This sounds a little dramatic, but after all, it was my first experience with my first teenager. I then prayed that if and when he came home, I would know how to show him my love amidst all the anger. I wanted to do this just right. He walked in the door, quickly apologized for making me worry and losing the sleep he knew I desperately needed. Then he said, "Mom, we need to talk."

For the first time in my life that I remember, I didn't say a word. I sat and listened. He told me how grateful he was for his friends and their standards, how he loved his high school, even what a great influence Principal Hawkins was on his life. The evening had been spent talking, and they lost track of time. (Has this ever happened to me?) These girls shared how they felt great pressure to abandon their personal standards. They didn't understand how to have a good time without breaking God's laws and commandments. He expressed his love to me for his family and his best friend, Shane. Then he mumbled, "I'm tired; I'm going to bed."

Like many significant moments in motherhood, this night is lost to my son's memory, but I will never forget it. It was very much against my nature to handle the situation as I did. I had asked for help and for once was smart enough to listen to the answer. I never did know who the girls were, but I was so grateful that through my patience I got to know my son better. Without jumping to conclusions about his irresponsibility and being inconsiderate, I was able to listen to his spirit. I felt wise. He was the teacher and I had been taught.

One young friend lamented that no matter how legitimate her reason for being late, her father would meet her at the door and yell in anger, "I don't want to hear your stupid excuses. Get straight to bed and you're grounded for two weeks." She would sleep miserably and in her teenage logic vow to be even later next time. Thus the battle began.

Other experienced parents have concluded with me that one of the best times to talk with teenagers is after midnight. The child is too tired to be very defensive, and there are no interruptions from phones or siblings. (I must admit that this gets harder as I get older.)

Another great time for open communication is during drive time. Many memorable teaching moments happen in the car. It seems that my children have perfected the art of raising their hands when anyone asks, "Whose mom can drive?" (And who says they're not talented?) While driving, I am privy to what my kids and their friends are thinking, and if I'm considered really cool they'll forget I'm there and I'll get to hear the good stuff. Parents who relinquish this opportunity really do miss out. Where better can I see what influences their daily lives? When I drive alone with a child, I turn off the radio and we just talk. Some of the most precious times I had with a busy, involved teenage daughter was Saturday mornings at 7:00 A.M. during the drive to Salt Lake City for piano lessons. She often expresses that she remembers more about the rides than the lessons. In fact, as happy as I am to have a teenager who can drive, I miss that rite of passage. Next to nursing a baby there is no greater feeling of being desperately needed than by a fifteen-and-a-half-year-old without wheels.

Listening carefully to your children not only makes them feel valued, it helps you to really know them. Anyone who has more than one child appreciates how different each one comes. Our summons as mothers is to acknowledge and validate that individuality. How do we do that? We spend the time it takes to get acquainted. Communication brings powerful knowledge. I've often thought that when I get to heaven, I would know my disabled child, Brady, because of his strong spirit and distinct personality, not because of his looks. They will continue to change as his disease progresses. What an interesting challenge to mothers everywhere—to know each child by his or her spirit!

Part of listening involves action. We must be humble and teachable. Changing your mind and adjusting to children's needs doesn't have to be viewed as wishy-washy or spineless. Aren't we placed here on earth to learn and grow? Adapting to a better way of doing things is progress. It takes humility on a parent's part to say, "Yup, you may be right about this one." I find my children are right a lot of the time. They are more often than not the teacher. Sometimes we may need to hear things that are painful or worrisome. A child may share hurt feelings over a lost campaign or broken engagement, stuff that is emotionally draining and that we can't do anything about. It is difficult to hear and not internalize their anguish. However, if you overreact to "not-such-great-news," the child will learn to lie and just tell you what you want to hear. They won't tell you about the fender bender or the drive in the muddy mountains. You'll just have to be surprised when you see the car in the morning.

Teenagers will oftentimes say things just to get you going. We have this running gag at our house when B.J., 16 and a constant kidder, tells me how fast he can drive to school. I shut my eyes and say, "I don't think I want to hear this." Whenever I ask him where he is going, his first answer is always Northern Exposure, a local bar. After I remind him that he went there last week and he is only allowed there once a month, then he tells me where he is really going.

Warning! There is a notable exception to all of the previous advice. There are times to not listen at all, just pretend. I could win an Academy Award with some of my performances. It takes great skill and knowledge to know exactly when that is. That time is when your child tells you something outlandish and impossible, such as when they want to buy an airplane or drive their friends in the new car, dragging a boat to Lake Powell the very week they get their driver's license. One daughter planned a rough-out hike in the wilderness with a bunch of girls who had no knowledge of how to camp. Plans that really are out of touch with reality usually have a way of dissolving themselves. I seldom have to put the kibosh on many excursions. I just pretend I am listening, smile, and say, "That sounds really fun." It's easy when you practice a lot. Deep down inside you know that there is no way that they can fulfill most of these designs, but everyone needs dreams (even if they are more like fantasies). I hear grandiose schemes and remember mine of my youth, dreams of sky diving and joining the Peace Corps. This method of "selective ignorance" saves a lot of confrontation over things that will never come to realization.

I think it is important that you respect kids' feelings when they tell you how they feel. I try to never say, "You shouldn't feel that way." If they do, they do. Once when my oldest was five, he announced that he hated me and was going to run away. I quickly told him that because he was such a great kid, I would help find him a good home. We got out the neighborhood list, and I read him the names of all the adults that he would have had contact with. After exhausting the entire list, he threw his arms around me and pronounced me the best mom ever.

A child's feelings are his own, but acting them out is a separate issue. Your children may not like everyone. That's okay. They may have a teacher or acquaintance who annoys them. I let them express these emotions, but I also expect them to treat everyone kindly and with respect. Everyone needs a place to be honest and unconditionally accepted. Listening in our homes is the best avenue to provide this place for healthy venting.

Probably the most important part of communicating in parenting is listening to the Holy Ghost. Respecting the gift of the Holy Ghost and acting upon those promptings is like developing spiritual muscles. The more you use it, the easier it is to recognize the help it offers for each of us. This listening, on more than one occasion, has saved my life. When I drive, I am usually thinking about and doing as many other things as possible. I try to efficiently file my nails or drink my eight glasses of water while cruising down the road at sixty miles an hour. Years ago, as a mother uneducated about yet-to-be-passed child car seat and seat belt laws, I would carry my babies on the seat next to me in a baby carrier. One day a voice filled the car and told me to be very careful. I pulled over and sat the baby carrier on the floor. I turned off the radio and proceeded with both hands on the wheel, totally focused on my driving. Not five minutes later a large telephone installation van pulled out in front of me from the left, leaving me two choices. I could swerve right and smack into the freeway entrance sign or veer left and chance going off the mountainside. I slammed on my brakes as hard as possible, swerving to the right onto the shoulder of the road and back up just in time to miss the sign. I pulled off at the next exit and screeched to a stop. I was badly shaken. The van driver pulled over beside me to see if I was all right. He profusely apologized and explained that I was in his blind spot and he had no idea I was even on the road. I was so grateful for this warning from the Holy Ghost; to this day I can never explain this experience away as coincidence.

I have had intuitions and spiritual help raising my family, which I have appreciated, but one time was especially significant. I had five brothers and sisters, but we were spread apart in age and I never felt like there were enough of us. I always wanted a large family and unabashedly announced to all my dates that I planned to have a dozen children (another one of those fantasy things). I also wondered why I didn't get many second dates. After the delivery of our first child lasted 24 hours, I thought Burke would be an only child. Six children later, I found myself perfectly satisfied (satiated may be a better description).

We were very surprised to find our family expecting an eighth child. I was always very sick for the first four months of every pregnancy, so friends and family would ask, "How can you do this again?" They thought I was being courageous or inordinately spiritual, when actually I had a short-term memory concerning pregnancy and long-term when it came to the pure pleasure of a baby in my home. With this baby I was sicker than ever, barely able to lift my head off the couch. It was December, and with two birthdays and Christmas coming, this was not at all a convenient time to be ill. One night I had a dream in black and white (I think that I normally dream in color). It had "Doc" from the old television show *Gunsmoke* examining my leg. He had a saw in his hands and I heard him talk about amputation. I woke my husband up and said that we needed to go to the hospital. I wanted to go to a trauma center and I was determined to stay, no matter what. Steve suggested that we wait at least until sunlight. He thought going in the middle of the night was a little dramatic. I had a feeling of foreboding and insisted on going immediately. When we arrived at LDS Hospital in Salt Lake City, the triage nurse asked me for a description of my symptoms. I felt a little foolish saying that I had had a dream and that, besides the excessive nausea that was normal for me, nothing else seemed wrong. She took me into the examining room and gave me skimpy hospital gown to slip on. Taking one look at my leg, she ordered, "Do not move; lay down!" and ran for the doctor. My left leg was swollen, purple, and suddenly very hot. He brought a measuring tape and found that one leg was two inches bigger around than the other—immediately he called in a peripheral vascular technician. Without having to beg to stay, I was informed that I would be their guest for several weeks and not to even raise my head off the bed. I had a three-foot blood clot that the study showed was down to my ankle and as close to my heart as the ultrasound waves could show. He informed my husband that if I had not come in, I would most likely be dead by noon. Talk about *me* being dramatic! (I just love it when I'm right.)

I was carefully watched over by a wonderful internist, Dr. Hal Cole, and a very supportive ObGyn, Dr. Kent Rasmussen. The surgeon, however, strongly suggested that I have an abortion. The last four babies had been born by means of a cesarean section, and my clotted condition would require me to be on blood thinner for the remainder of the pregnancy. If I were to go into an unscheduled labor, I would hemorrhage. My life was in jeopardy.

The choice was easy after an ultrasound revealed a perfectly healthy active baby waving hello to her daddy. After fifteen days in the hospital I returned home just before Christmas.

It wasn't until several months later than I discovered the connection between my dream and my blood clot. I was required to have blood drawn every other day to determine its thickness and, based on those results, give myself between three and eight shots of heparin a day. I had volunteered to give a ride to a new acquaintance who was in community theater with my son. When she got in the car and saw my needles and medication, she said, "Oh, you must have a blood clot. I had a blood clot they couldn't dissolve, and I came within one day of having my leg cut off." She explained that previous to

World War II, when heparin was discovered, the only remedy for blood clots was amputation. I had no knowledge of that. Academically my dream now made sense. Spiritually it had already saved my life.

I have learned not to ignore any promptings or warnings in my life. How would I dare? How could I raise my family? I certainly don't consider myself unique in the insights or help that I have had. The Holy Ghost is there for all of us. Listening to children, husband, or the Spirit is a skill that needs constant sharpening—it is never "done." The process is continuous and, oh, so rewarding.

Take Off the Robe:
You're Not the Judge

Introducing advice for soothing the pain
of being judged and strengthening your
resolve not to judge others

Here comes the judge!" The well-known comedic phrase from television history really strikes home when you are the recipient of the judgment. At one time, I took quite a bit of pride in thinking myself a nonjudgmental person. How wrong I was! It was not until I was the recipient of being wrongfully judged that I really understood the wisdom in this counsel and the heartache we render when we sinfully judge others. "Judge not, that ye be not judged" (Matthew 7:1; see also vv. 2–5) is simple, strong, sound advice. Everyone is familiar with the age-old adage, "Don't judge a man until you've walked a mile in his moccasins." Instead vow, "I won't judge at all; my own feet hurt, and I don't want to wear your dang shoes."

Everyone at one time or another has been wrongfully judged. Discreet neighbors and friends will usually keep their opinions to themselves, unless they share them with others who agree not to reveal them to you. Even then such judging is harmful. Those doing the scrutinizing lose their sense of compassion, charity, and understanding. Judging that is felt by others harms both parties.

I want to share with you my Garbage Can Theory. First, let me give you some background about myself. After seven years with no babies in the house, my parents were thrilled with my expected arrival. Born on the Fourth of July, I was greeted by a nine-year-old sister and seven-year-old twin sisters who absolutely worshiped me. I was their baby. They showered me with attention and doted on me. I remember thinking that the parades and fireworks celebrating our country's birthday were actually for me. I guess I had what in modern terms would be considered great self-esteem. I would do anything for attention, including standing on my head in the corner for hours just to impress home teachers (maybe I should consider resorting to this method again). I needed to be front row at the dance recitals (that was easy because I was short) and wanted constant validation.

This insatiable craving for attention and approval carried over into my adult life and soon became a problem. My husband did not appreciate my antics the way my six college roommates did, and, as most mothers know, motherhood is a reward in itself, i.e., no one gives a hoot about you anymore. (Just kidding.)

Midlife brought to me a special reward—I lost the craving for approval. It's almost fun, and no longer discouraging, to think, "Oh, what the heck. I can't please them anyway; I'll do it my way." This works equally well with husbands, children, neighbors, and innocent passers-by, especially when planning menus or outings. In fact, people who don't adapt to this philosophy of not caring what others think will often end up either institutionalized or heavily medicated. Seriously.

Everyone has their own path to this liberation, but mine began with garbage cans, hence the Garbage Can Theory. In my city the garbage collection is automated. The city rents homeowners huge 90-gallon rubber refuse containers with flip-top lids. Every house is assigned one, with an additional charge for any extra cans. The week's garbage is then collected by large noisy trucks (I've decided they're loud to remind you to take the garbage out). The trucks lumber down each side of the street, pausing just long enough for big metal hydraulic arms to grab the can, lift it, dump it, and toss it back into your yard within seconds. Our can was filled within three days and I knew we needed a second one. No problem. Call the city, they deliver. Five days into the week both cans are full. We needed a third. My son Brady is on a respirator that requires circuit changes every 48 hours. This involves yards of flexible blue tubing plus sterilizing procedures that produce an enormous amount of refuse. Some days it seems to approach that of a small hospital. I called the city and sheepishly requested a third garbage can. The next Thursday, I took the garbage out to the street, jumped in the car to drive my shift in the car pool, and counted the garbage cans on the way to the junior high. We were the only family I could see within miles that had three garbage cans. I wondered what people would think. Were we indulgent, spoiled, materialistic, rich? I was driving home and the absurdity hit me; I actually braked, then laughed out loud. Who would have absolutely nothing to do but count garbage cans, *and* if they did, why would I care about their opinion? It was so liberating. I found freedom in my new truth. My Garbage Can Theory goes like this: who cares about the opinion of those who have nothing better to do than to care about things that do not matter?

I have found that I need to ultimately care what my Father in Heaven thinks. I run problems past him in prayer, and, with the help of the Holy Ghost, I make my decision. If he's square with it and I know in my heart I'm right, then even my husband's approval isn't necessary for confirmation. Let me give you an example. Our disabled son, Brady, was five years old, and we were anticipating his entrance into kindergarten the next year. That spring I was called by a PTA volunteer to participate in a workshop at school to educate children about various disabilities. I had this great idea to take Brady along so everyone could meet him (sort of like a visual aid). I excitedly explained my plan to my husband, Steve, and expected he would think that was great. (I want him to think all my ideas are great.) He did not like the idea at all. Steve has always been proud to be Brady's dad, and he was very skeptical that this would be good for Brady. He did not want him to be a spectacle or gawked at. I was insulted that he would even think that I would want that for Brady. He did, however, bring up a few good points. He was rather firm that I not do this workshop. I honestly considered his counsel, went to the Lord with what to do, and then made up my mind. I knew that I should.

I began the workshop by describing a small, slimy creature with very long skinny fingers; he didn't talk normally and had large, buggy eyes. He would repeat the same phrase over and over, yet all the kids loved this creature. His name was E.T. The movie by the same name had just been released and was a smashing success. Children don't notice differences like adults do and are willing to love and accept unquestionably. I told the children that Brady didn't speak normally; he walked with a very gaited walk and was wobbly. His eyes didn't open wide—he wore glasses and a patch over his left eye. He couldn't stand up if he fell down, and he would never run or ride a bike. I stood with him in front of the children and told them about his sense of humor, all the things he liked to eat, his favorite television programs, and his family. I told them that Brady already had many friends and that he loved people. I invited his friends to stand, thinking that I would give recognition to those who already knew him. Suddenly all the children in the room jumped to their feet. Every child there thought I meant him or her. I cried. The principal cried. The teachers cried. There was not a dry eye of any adult in that room. It was one of the most special days of mine and Brady's life. The principal immediately notified the district that Brady would be coming and asked us what would be necessary to accommodate him. We, as his parents, got a foot in the door for the uphill battle involving school. I knew it was the right thing to do; I am so glad I did it.

You may wonder what judging has to do with mothering? It is all encompassing. A judgmental person feels like everyone else is also judgmental. It restricts your vision and growth. I think that it leads to an insecurity that undermines your God-given skills to nurture. Leading child-rearing experts frequently advise, "When in doubt, follow your instincts." These instincts become skewed when you inordinately worry about what others may think of you.

Not judging is a lifelong skill that needs constant practice. There may be days or even years, depending on your own circumstances, when you may hold back your opinion, but slowly the urge to pass judgment comes back. This thorn of unrighteousness needs constant clipping.

What seems hardest is to not judge the very person judging you. One day a stranger knocked on my door, hysterically screaming at me about children in the road. I couldn't even understand her rambling as I followed her waving arms held high out into the street to see my six-year-old and two-year-old walking hand in hand up the street. They seemed perfectly fine to me. She demanded to know if they were my children; when I claimed them, she just ripped into me about leaving them unattended outside. I stayed calm. She ranted on about them walking in the street (there are no sidewalks around that corner). She wanted to know what was wrong with me and if I was crazy. (I wanted to tell her that the jury was still out on that one, but I didn't think she'd appreciate my humor.) The more agitated she became, the louder she yelled. I stayed calm. She didn't wait for any response. She just ran to her car that she had left running in the middle of the street with the door open (that didn't seem so safe to me either!) and sped off. I quizzed the girls to see if this lady had almost hit them or had to swerve or what, but they did not have any idea what I was talking about. They just said that she had stopped and asked them where they lived.

A few hours later, I got a call from the Bountiful police seeking an interview with me to investigate me for child abuse. This lady had called the police and demanded an inquiry. She explained that I wasn't upset with the children in the street or with her. She thought that I must be emotionally unattached and therefore abusive. Then I was angry. I told the officer that he didn't need an appointment, that he was welcome anytime, but he needed to understand that I had a chronically ill son dependent on a respirator. I had been through many near-death experiences with him being disabled all his life, and between meeting his medical needs and trying to mother the other seven children that I indeed was emotionally spent. (I secretly thought a few days in jail sounded very peaceful. I envisioned myself demanding solitary confinement and a good book, refusing even the one phone call I was allowed. I thought I could see the headlines of the local paper now, "Newly Awarded Young Mother of the Year Gets the Slammer." I also wondered if I could get the stripes of the prison uniforms to go vertical, which would be far more flattering than horizontal ones.) I gave the officer a few references to call and never heard from him again. I probably have a record somewhere.

I got madder and madder as the day went on, and when my husband came home I let him have it (that's what husbands are for). "How dare she judge me, how dare she question my mothering skills, or my judgment! She didn't even bother finding out that I couldn't retrieve my two-year-old from the babysitter's because I couldn't leave Brady on the ventilator. Just plain, how dare she!" Steve listened to the whole tirade and calmly put his arm around me. "Don't judge her, Earlene. She may have had a child die in a car accident, or maybe hit a child herself with her car, or not be able to have children at all. You just don't know where she is coming from; you may not understand." I was no different from her— I was doing the same thing to this unknown woman that I had hated being done to me. I was judging her. I immediately was grateful for Steve's wisdom.

Living under constant criticism is demeaning to the spirit. Husbands, wives, and siblings who constantly berate each other are harming the whole divine system of families. I have a situation in my home where I fall under intense scrutiny daily. After Brady had spent four months in intensive care at the hospital, the insurance company was frantically looking for ways to get Brady out of the hospital and

home. The doctors agreed that he could be one of the first pe-
diatric patients in Utah to be on a ventilator at home—provided that he had 24-hour nurse's care for a few months, or at
least until his condition was stable. Every eight hours a different nurse would be in our home with our family. Home
nursing was also a new concept, so everyone was learning. I
was trying to please each nurse. I wanted them to feel at
home and to like me and my "perfect" little family so they
would deliver the best care for my son. I was changing personalities and rules every shift in order to adapt to each
nurse's expectations. After a while, nurses felt comfortable
enough to help me out with little suggestions like how to cook
my food, identifying which child was a "brat," indicating
where to shop for groceries and what clothes to wear. One
day after my hanging a new picture on the wall, the nurse
said in passing, "By the way, I don't like that picture." Another time after hitting a great sale (my favorite hobby) and
purchasing all the kids' next summer's clothes for 75 percent
off, the nurse took my husband aside and told him that he
was married to a spendthrift. She had been through the children's drawers and found out that the clothes were not even
their sizes. After Steve jokingly conveyed this conversation to
me in bed that night, I berated him for not having defended
me. I was wrong for doing so. He was already where I needed
to go: he knew that I was very frugal and, besides that, what
did he care what the nurse thought of me. I still didn't like
her very much.

Brady loved Cub Scouts and was adored by the whole
ward, so when Steve was out of town the night we had pack
meeting, I arranged for a nurse to accompany me. Brady
needed suction during the drive and always required an
older sibling, nurse, or dad along. I also had a six-, four-, and
two-year-old tagging along. (After all, pack meeting is a family affair. As a side note, I cannot tell you how thrilled I am
that our last two children are girls. I have had fifteen consecutive years of Cub Scouts and know every kind of applause

available.) The pack meeting had displays all around the gym, so Brady and I went from table to table to view everyone's projects. He really enjoyed it but tired quickly, so we left early to come home.

After we got him settled in his room, the nurse said that she wanted to talk to me. She told me that I was the most selfish, inconsiderate person that she had ever met. I was stunned! Didn't she know how my family all adored me? Didn't she know that I lived to please? I couldn't even begin to understand what she was talking about. I thought we had had a great evening. Brady had been so happy, so included, and so normal. She went on to explain that I had left her sitting on a folding chair without anyone to talk to; she didn't know anyone there, and she hadn't felt involved. She suggested that I consider leaving Brady home on family excursions.

I was in shock and didn't know what to say for a long time. I slowly gathered my composure and admitted to her that Brady had been my only concern, then I just turned and walked away. I felt bad for her. She was a very insecure, sad person. Another nick in my self-esteem. Another lesson to be learned. My instincts had been right, however, so despite how hurt I was, I never for a moment considered her advice. Brady lived to be with his family and friends. It was all he had. Without Steve to hear me out, I prayed. I prayed for forgiveness if I needed it (which may not have been very sincere because I was sure I didn't) and for comfort. I immediately felt better. I needed to learn again to set aside egos and not internalize hurts or self-doubts. Moms need to be good at shrugging off criticism. It that were an Olympic event, I would be a gold medal contender.

Because I had seven children under eleven years old, I also employed a part-time nanny to help give the other kids all the attention they needed, or so I planned. One day a lady in the ward commented, "Wow, you have a nanny and a nurse; how does it feel to be a lady of leisure?" I nearly lost it.

It took a baptism by fire and years of journey to decide who I am and where I am going. I felt very much like a convert to the Church, searching for the truth, only to learn that I had had it all along. Unlike the worldly advice of pleasing yourself, the key is simple: please God. Know him well enough to know what he wants and expects—then do it. Criticism is hurtful to everyone involved, and the longer I live the more grateful I am to God that he doesn't require or want me to judge others.

It is true that you can't please all of the people all of the time. Don't even try. Just concentrate on pleasing the One who really counts.

Just Say No to Saying No

Suggesting a remedy for those who feel their negativism is in need of treatment

Just Say No!"

I'm all for it as an antidrug message, but when parenting I try to avoid saying no whenever possible. This advice may be contrary to what most people accept as good parenting. It may be even considered revolutionary. After all, who is in control here?

That is my very point! Parenting isn't about control. Whether you believe it or not, when it comes to a power of wills, the parents will always lose in the end; after all, they are older and worn out. Try outwaiting a five-year-old, or try saying no just one more time than a two-year-old can say yes. Even if the child seems compliant at the time, he may just be clever enough to have fooled you into thinking that you have won. I have had a ton of teenagers in my home (see, I even talk like them), and I swear it's true. Kids behave however they choose in the absence of parental scrutiny. I have had far too many experiences being a youth leader when the absolute "worst" child was the one from a strict, rigid family. The child, who was very obedient at home, would go ballistic when finally let out. The trick is getting them to *want* to act appropriately with or without parental supervision.

I am no expert on child rearing, just experienced. So far, I have had seven teenagers of my own and a niece that lived with us for two years. When I'm done (are you ever done?), I will have clocked in twenty-four consecutive years of raising teenagers (if I survive that long). I realize that is not material for the *Guinness Book of Records*, but at least I know more than I did twenty years ago. Thank heaven! I also acknowledge that one kind of teenager can be harder than ten others. Keep in mind that I also understand that I am not done raising my own (that is the scary thing about giving anyone advice about anything). Because every child is different, every experience will be.

In our family, we don't have a lot of rules. We jokingly brag at our house that we only have one rule, "Don't bleed on the carpet." We try to say no very rarely. (Our children would tell you this is totally untrue, that we say no all the time.) The effectiveness of this idea may prove to be arguable—depending on your own experience. My mother didn't agree with me for years. She had a rule for everything, as I think most moms in my generation did. On the other hand, other parents who have numerous problems with their adolescent children lament, "I just wasn't strict enough." Face it, parenting can often feel like a no-win situation. Sometimes we never know if what we did was right or wrong for that child, but I do feel that our family philosophy seems to work for us and for many other families. I have many friends with nice, decent, hardworking, obedient children that have few restrictions. This may take some practice at first. Don't be frightened. I consider my parenting style rather traditional in terms of expectations and liberal in acceptance. We are not talking about carte blanche behavior here with overly permissive absentee parents. We are simply talking about letting the adolescent call a few more of the shots—govern themselves, as it were.

If possible when addressing a request from a child, I like to say yes, even if it is a qualified yes. For example, I might say, "What a great idea, but this weekend is not possible. How about Thursday next week?" The child may still be disappointed, but if it was impossible anyway it gives them hope. It is important though to follow through next Thursday. That makes you dependable, just like you want them to be. Children want choices like everyone else; the more choices they are allowed as children, the better skills they will have as adults. Parents who tell their children exactly what, when, where, and how to do things are left wondering why that same child, years later, can't make a decision or why he just follows the crowd. In fulfilling their need for independence, teenagers will sometimes not ask permission at all, especially if they think that you will say no. I've never met a teenager yet who hasn't done something that their parents don't know about. That is natural and to be accepted and expected. I also believe that if you say yes 90 percent of the time, they will respect the 10 percent turndowns because they believe you must have a really good reason.

When a child—or even husband—asks you to do something that you're not sure about or needs some research, don't say no immediately. Instead say, "Let me think about it." This may sound like extra work or that you are setting yourself up to be nagged, which is all true, but it also sets up the situation for you to say yes if after evaluation you find it possible. If the answer is still no, they will have to accept it, but you are not locked into sticking by your guns just to show you are right.

My sister knew I was attempting to write this chapter and told me I must include our experience at the art fair. I didn't even know that she had observed me using this theory. In fact, I didn't even know it was a theory until I wrote about it. I just know that for my family it appears to be working (I'm keeping in mind that "I'm not done" thing). My sister and I had taken a Korean visitor, three of my children, and three of their friends to the Salt Lake Arts Festival. This was a fun place to see various artistic styles and observe artsy people. There were lots of things for the younger children to do and dozens of booths displaying art, jewelry, and clothing for sale. The twelve-year-old (almost thirteen, as she always adds) started begging me to come see this incredible clay jewelry several booths away. I had a pretty good idea the price was unreachable, since this was a fair to which you came to appreciate the artistic skills, not a place to shop for a family of ten. I said, "Sure, let's go see it." Bobbie Jo picked up her favorite piece of black-and-taupe beaded bracelet and, looking up with soft eyes, pleaded, "Can I have this?" "Well, let's see how much it is," I replied. "Seventy-two dollars," the clerks spoke up. I put my arm around Bobbie Jo, leaned in close, and asked, "Exactly how many should we buy?" We all had a good laugh over that. The word no was never mentioned. Needless to say, we did not buy the bracelet or anything else that day. Everyone went home happy and I forgot about the whole thing.

My sister said that as she replayed the scenario in her mind on her drive home, she imagined how she might have handled that situation. She says she would have refused to go look at the bracelet at all because she knew she wouldn't buy it. If she did look, she would have said no before even asking the price, *and* if she knew the price she would have said, "Absolutely not! If I spend $72 on you, then the other three kids would expect me to spend that on them, and that is ridiculous. Do you know how much four times $72 is? You would probably just lose it anyway."

Same results—no bracelet purchased. The first scenario told the child, "Your taste and interests are important to me, and if you desire something, at least inquire about it. You never know—some things are possible." The second example would leave Mom mad that the child was so foolish to have even wanted the bracelet, and the child would confirm that Mom is just a grouch: "She always says no anyway, and she thinks I don't take care of my stuff."

There is an old story about a reporter who asked an old Jewish woman in an interview, "Why do Jews always answer a question with a question?" She answered, "Why not?" Try replacing no with a question when answering a child. This makes the child an inquisitive person, and many experts feel like it raises their intellect. At the very least, it makes the child think for himself. One day while we were waiting in a long line at a Sears catalogue store, my five-year-old saw a display of rubber bacon and eggs sitting in a new frying pan. He immediately asked, "Are those real?" Instead of saying no and being done with it, I said, "What do you think?" His reply, "I don't think so." I asked, "Why don't you think so?" After further examination he said, "Because I think I couldn't chew them and they don't smell good; I think they are fake." "Good answer," I replied. "I think asking lots of questions and figuring things out on your own makes for a smart young man." He beamed. I may have overdone it because the last child is very annoying to her brothers, asking constant questions. I often hear her sass back, "I can ask anything I want. Mom says that makes me smart." If they don't bodily harm her first, I think it will.

Just yesterday in a department store, I observed an expectant mother with two children in tow. (Brave woman to even come to the store.) The oldest, about four years old, lifted up the lid on a large cooking pot to see what was in it. She said, "Cameron, if you set that lid down and look into the top, you'll see your reflection. Do you know what a reflection is? Isn't that shiny?" He looked into the chrome lid, pulled a few faces to see how strange he looked, and went on his way. She never said, "Set that lid down *now*! I'm warning you! Don't you know when you come to the store you don't touch things? How many times do I have to tell you? I'm not going to bring you to the store again if you have to constantly touch everything. If every child who passed that pot lifted that lid up and down, it would be broken and nobody would want to buy it." Sound at all familiar? Sometimes when I am around a mother who lectures so much, I'm tired of her rambling in a few minutes. I can't imagine what it's like for the child every day. Adults often just talk too much.

Often when a child deserves a legitimate punishment, I ask him what he would do if he were the parent. He will usually come up with an appropriate restriction, sometimes one that I would not have thought of. The interesting thing is how he feels more committed to follow through. One of the smaller boys decided to ground himself from the skateboard. After two days he asked if he couldn't please get it back. I reminded him that he chose to give it up, not me. Try as he may, he could not blame me. He grudgingly followed through with his own punishment. Attempt this for a few weeks with your family and see if the conflict isn't lessened in your home. Catch yourself when you slip into the lecture mode, ask a question, and just sit back and listen. Your children may surprise you; they are smarter than you might think.

I Went Kicking and Screaming
All the Way . . . to Work

Medicating the reality and pain of
mothers who have to work

When my fourth child, Brady, was born with a rare, unidentified disease, temporarily labeled "floppy baby," the insurance world gave us a big thumbs down. Overnight, we became one of those dreaded "uninsurables." It sounds like one of those obscure diseases where nobody dares touch you. In the case of the insurance carriers, that was true.

After ten years of being a responsible young couple carrying life, homeowners, automobile, and medical insurance—including maternity—we were put on notice. Our bills were closely monitored, and the insurance premiums doubled every year. After several years the company threatened to drop us completely. I called the Utah State Insurance Commission and found that because we had private insurance (a single policy), that was perfectly legal. My husband was self-employed and did not have the luxury of "hiding" in a large insurance pool. Those who work for large companies who have handicapped children become job-locked. They can rarely be insured on a new company's policy, so they have to stay put. Even worse, those employed by small companies are often dismissed because the premiums for the whole group are raised so high that they become unreachable for all the other employees.

We were desperate. Besides Brady's potential for astronomical bills, by then we had seven other children to cover. I called the insurance commission back, pleading for advice. They said I had several options. All of them included my going to work. "Hey," I wanted to argue. "I do work, and darn hard," but I think they meant somewhere where I would get paid. They suggested that I work at a very large corporation and identified the three largest employers in the state. The school districts, the LDS Church, and the hospital systems. We have since learned of other solutions that couples like us have resorted to. Divorce was one option—we jokingly admitted that it sounded pretty good to share custody with alternate weeks "alone." Welfare was another. Steve employed fifty-four people at that time, which meant putting all their families out of work. Furthermore, I think my workaholic husband would have made a very cranky unemployed person. Making Brady a ward of the state was another alternative. We have since met families who have had to make one or more of those choices for survival.

Upon further research, I found that the insurance for LDS Church employees has a two-year waiting period for preexisting conditions. The school district required full-time employment with a six-month wait, so I focused on the hospital systems. They only required 24 hours a week to qualify for insurance. They also would cover preexisting conditions within six months or two thousand dollars, whichever came first. Brady qualified in ten days.

I realize my working mother experience isn't typical, nor was it as burdensome as most. I have met many mothers with more children than I have, who work longer, harder hours and sometimes have no spouse at home. My heart goes out to them, along with my respect. But for me, this was traumatic. I loved being home and was never bored. I am weird and unusual because I like doing laundry and driving car pools. I wanted to cry every night. I felt so bad for myself. It wasn't my choice—I was cornered, I had no alternative. I wasn't going to be there when the kids got home. I would miss holidays and bedtimes. I hated the idea. I think in this way, I am very typical. I know there are exceptions, but most of my working mom friends feel the same way. I learned there are many moms who have to work; they also don't have a lot of choices.

I had the luxury all those years at home of working with people I loved and found an eternal purpose in even the most mundane of my tasks. I now needed to get into the "real" world. I was resentful but also scared. Who would hire me? I had never typed a resume in my life. My last job paid $1.25 an hour and was twenty years ago. My confidence wavered like a seismograph during an earthquake. I told myself, "I have a college education." Then another voice reminded me that my degree was in social work and without a master's degree and experience, it meant nothing in the employment line. I reasoned that it might be fun to wear makeup, nylons, and hairspray all at the same time. I could get in the car and drive to work, leaving my troubles behind. (I can hear you chuckling now.) Instead, my worries and work just followed me around and multiplied when I wasn't looking. I was afraid of rejection. There was a really good chance someone wouldn't want me to work for them. I put in applications for every job available at several hospitals. I was willing to work any shift at any skill level. Since I knew they wouldn't hire me as an administrator, I just hoped the laundry service job didn't come through. It looked really hot.

I applied at the emergency room for a unit clerk position. But before they called me in for an interview, I needed to quickly learn what a unit clerk was. In all my experience with hospitals, I hadn't yet met one. I found that I first needed to pass a six-week course, including medical terminology, and have experience. I hurriedly signed on for the class, doubled up on assignments, and finished in three weeks. Then I went for my interview. (I would worry about experience later.) I didn't even know what to wear, but I did comb my hair and arrive early. The department supervisor said that before she asked me any questions she wanted to give me a description of the position. It was not a job for the faint of heart. I naively thought she meant because of blood and messy accidents. I was wrong. She said every shift was chaotic—the phone rings constantly and ambulance radio calls go off in the background. I would have to decipher doctors' handwriting that even they couldn't. I would have enormous responsibility and no authority. I would get yelled at for things that were not my fault. I must deal with a multitude of personalities and temperaments, most of which would not be easy. There were no "coffee breaks" in an emergency setting, and meals were unheard of, except on the run. I would get no credit if things ran smoothly and all the blame if they didn't. I nearly jumped out of my seat with excitement. This was a job I'd trained for all my life. "Sounds just like home," I explained. I was hired on the spot.

Juggling things at home will always be the hardest part of employed mothers. Some things just had to go. It was time to evaluate priorities. All mothers eventually have to do this, working or not. Homemade goodies, ironing, and every meal "made from scratch" was hard for this Cache Valley girl to give up. When I was a child we had even made our own soap and bought our chickens live. I had never bought a box of Stove Top Stuffing or Betty Crocker prepared frosting. I was also PTA president at the high school and a Laurel adviser in our ward. I had to make some serious adjustments. At work, I didn't socialize after hours, so for the first time in my life, I felt like "odd man out." People at work from other departments would come by my desk just to see this "woman with eight kids." Even in downtown Salt Lake City I was considered an oddity. Co-workers were fascinated with stories of my home life, usually accompanied by looks of bewilderment or sympathy. They would ask me funny questions like, "How do you cook French toast for so many? Do you drink real milk?" At least I was good for some comedic relief. When they commented that work must be a great break for me, I still just wanted to cry inside. I wanted to be home.

Those feelings aside, I *chose* to work on Sundays. Steve could be home with the kids, I reasoned. Besides, if he was alone with all eight he could see how hard it really was. Talk about guilt! I was a working mom, working on Sundays, *and*, for a triple scoop of contrition, found it easier than being home.

When the staff divided holidays, I quickly volunteered for New Year's Eve, and then begrudgingly had to also accept Christmas Eve. If they only knew how fun those nights were at my house, they would have shut the hospital down. Thanksgiving was my first holiday to work. It wasn't so bad at work, not many accidents, everyone fairly cheerful, and Steve home cooking a full-course dinner for ten. The family waited patiently (ha ha) for me to finish my shift, and we ate at four in the afternoon. After everyone had wolfed down their meal in fifteen minutes and hurriedly left the table, Steve just sat there stunned. He looked at all the dishes, then the kitchen, and said, "I just don't think it's worth it; I cooked for eight hours and nobody cared." I loved it. It turned out to be a great holiday.

I had to work for only five years until Brady was eighteen and could be insured by the state, but the lessons I learned will always be there. I will not judge but will always support my working friends. I will drive more than my share of car pools. I will have a home other children can come to in the morning or after school if they need a place to be. I will mother as many children around me as possible. I will do more than my share in the community. I will never criticize Church leaders who maybe don't have quite enough time for all their responsibilities. I will respect someone's ability to say no. I will never go a day without thanking my Father in Heaven in prayer and my husband in person for the great privilege I have to be home.

Service Is a Two-Way Street

Realizing that there is a remedy for life's difficulties no matter where you stand

My mother was probably the most service-oriented person I have ever known. She never considered anything too hard or inconvenient for her to do (or to get her kids to do). I grew up delivering home-baked goodies daily and never ate anything without first asking, "Is this for us?" My regular job was to set the table, and each time I would have to ask, "How many?" I seriously don't remember a Sunday meal without a guest or two. If no one was invited, Mom would find someone at church to bring home.

My mom was very clever—she could figure out more ways for us kids to work than anyone I knew. We could all make a batch of rolls by the time we were twelve and tended neighbor kids even when we had the measles. (It was believed that light was damaging to the eyes when you had the measles, so she would tie a dishcloth over our eyes and tell us to "get on over there to help.") Every Saturday, Mom used to go fix two elderly neighbors' hair, Grandma Low and Grandma Campbell. As a judgmental preadolescent I thought it was strange that Mom curled their hair when she sometimes forgot to fix her own. One day Mother was much too busy to go, so she sent me. I felt uncomfortable at first because I used brush curlers and picks and was afraid that I would poke their heads. Grandma Low was also deaf, so in order to carry on a conversation I had to shout. I soon became the Saturday designated hair curler. Interestingly enough, I learned to love my two adopted grandmas and felt really cool when I could invite friends to sit on their porch swings or invite them in for goodies. Grandma Low would even let me have sleepovers at her house. If you want a definition of a good time for a thirteen-year-old, it would be to have friends stay overnight at a deaf lady's house.

Years later I was sitting in Relief Society when they welcomed a new elderly member. Sister Larsen, eighty years old and in a wheelchair, had recently moved into her son's home. As I sat by this sweet sister, wonderful memories came flooding back from my childhood. I looked her over and decided that she needed me to do her hair. Being socially appropriate, I waited until I got home to call and offer my services. I told her that I missed my grandmas and that I needed her. She was probably wondering why I wanted to do her hair when mine didn't look so great. Anyway, we became best friends. She was fifty years and one day older than I was and had a wonderful sense of humor. She shared the best stories with me and my children (they took turns coming with me, so as not to overwhelm her). She had been an FBI spy, assigned to infiltrate the labor unions during World War II. She also had a handicapped son who didn't have the medical resources my son did and died at age 11 without ever having gone to school. She studied the gospel daily and shared with me her testimony and her life. We spent every Saturday together for a year and a half until she died. I still miss her.

As an adult, I see the gospel in action as life shaping, not just as performing good deeds. Self-esteem and confidence burst forward in huge bounds when children find themselves doing good. As a child, I felt confident in challenging situations, I knew a lot of adults, and I learned to love the elderly. Yesterday I went to deliver a neighbor's favorite pie and my youngest piped up, "Let me take it, Mom. Bill loves me." Déjà vu. Parents can often set up situations for success.

As I was driving the umpteenth car pool this week, a novel idea crossed my mind. I spend hundreds of hours and dollars each month so that my children can do back flips in front of cheering crowds, perform double somersaults off a diving board, hit people (football), kick people (soccer), play boogie woogie songs on the piano (he's supposed to be practicing hymns), and sing the latest Whitney Houston ballad. In the overall big picture, what I really want them to learn is kindness, courage, responsibility, and integrity. Why can't there be a school for this? A compassionate academy. Wouldn't it be great if we could drop the kids off at 4:00 and pick them up at 5:30, every Tuesday and Thursday, then politely inquire, "What did you learn today?" We could even have recitals. Costumes and uniforms would be simple, and shoes could be used for more than one season. I am being facetious because I know that such training is my job, but wouldn't that be easier? How many parents and kids would put that kind of time into something so intangible?

Our summer guest was a perfect example of this lesson. This past June my son returned home from the Taejon, Korean mission. Six days later, we had an unexpected visit from his favorite convert, Kim Myong Jay. We were a little unprepared because we forgot to tell the missionary that his oldest brother (along with wife, baby, and dog) moved back home two months before while they were building a new home. He forgot to tell us he had a guest arriving, so we were pretty even. It was a cozy five weeks with just the twelve of us. Summers are crazy anyway because of our family's lack of routine, and we had tried to show our guest as many sights as possible, but three days before Kim went home he had a dozen errands to run. That meant Mom to the rescue (the missionary had a job).

One hot afternoon I waited in the car forty minutes and was starting to get impatient, mostly with myself. I had so much to do at home. I saw Kim come out of the store with a big smile on his face. He had bought his father the perfect present. He was swinging hands and laughing with both my young girls. It hit me like a bolt of lightning. What could I do more important than this? My children loved Kim as he tried to teach them Korean. They shared their customs, food, books, music, and stories with him. He taught them about his previous Muslim religion and explained that he lost all his friends when he joined the LDS church. He loved my missionary son with real devotion and called me his American Mom. How could I put a price tag (or time tag) on this day? I want to teach the children tolerance for other religions, expose them to various cultures, and create self-confidence around other nationalities, yet I was irritated about a few minutes' wait? When will I ever learn? And guess what! When I got home, everything to be done was still there waiting for me.

It's easy to teach about service, it's harder to actually do it, but the hardest of all is to accept it. I am probably the world's expert on the receiving end. I think about all the good things people have done for me and it makes me very humble. If I listed all of the kindnesses done for me and my family, this book would have a volume two and volume three.

Each act I witness teaches me a new gospel principle. Henry Engh taught me to go the second mile. He was the high priest group leader (my husband was an elder), and he owned a large garden shop. He had to drive past my house to church and must have noticed my sad yard. In May one year, I broke my tailbone during delivery of my third child and could hardly walk. Besides the newborn, I had a twenty-month-old and a three-year-old to take care of. My husband worked six days a week until dark, so the yard suffered. I had planned a beautiful large flower garden, but it existed only in my mind.

One day a large flatbed truck backed into my driveway, three workers got out, and, with Henry personally supervising, they planted the most gorgeous, colorful garden possible. Unbeknownst to Henry, I had previously fertilized the area in hopes of future planting. I didn't really know how much to use and could never figure cubic feet anyway, so I just dumped the whole box and mixed it in the soil. I guess I over-did it. Within one week, the garden was all dead. I could not hide it—the garden was huge and smack in front of the house on a highly visible street. I thought I could put a tarp over it or just not go to church for the rest of the summer. Maybe we should just move. I really was embarrassed and didn't want to appear ungrateful. I needn't have worried. Henry came back again, unannounced, dug in some neutralizer, and re-planted the whole garden. Needless to say, we became life-long friends.

Many acts of kindness were from strangers or remained anonymous. When Brady had been hospitalized in Hawaii for four months and we needed to return to Utah, the hospital would not release him without a doctor accompanying us home, which meant an extra airplane ticket. Because the ambulance brought him directly to the airport, I didn't do his packing. We had every medical necessity anticipated for the eight-hour flight, but no one had thought to pack diapers. After we had been in the air several hours, we realized our dilemma. The flight attendant soon brought us several diapers from a nice couple in first class who were traveling with a baby Brady's same size. Soon after, I received a tap on the shoulder—there stood the famous singer Glen Campbell. He had come to check on Brady after donating his diapers. He was genuinely concerned for us as well as Brady.

Another time I had taken eight loads of wet clothes to the laundromat because the dryer just couldn't keep up (it was on its last legs). There were two other ladies and one young man also doing their wash. I was always overwhelmed with laundry and a little frazzled. I guess it showed. One lady asked me if I was okay. I admitted that I was never sure. I filled several of the large capacity dryers, shoved in the coins, and dashed out the door to go home and fix dinner. When I returned at nine, the doors were locked. I thought all laundromats were open twenty-four hours a day (they are in the movies). Even though it is more expensive, I had thought I just might start slipping down there in the middle of the night to get it all done at once. I then read the hours posted in big numbers on the door: 9 to 9. I made sure that I was there when the doors opened the next morning, after spending the night hoping someone hadn't stolen my family's clothes. I was the first one through the door, and was I surprised! There was all my laundry, nicely folded and stacked in piles ready to take home. I couldn't believe it; I have no idea who was so kind. This may not seem like much, but I will never forget it.

I have had meals prepared, driveways scraped, rides provided for children, and household repairs all done by loving neighbors. My sisters have helped me with babies (one flew in from Indianapolis for two weeks). My brother calls me every day just to check on me, and my oldest sister even potty trained half my children. Now, that's love! Brady's friends bring dance pictures and dates to our home so he feels included. When I was hospitalized with a life-threatening blood clot a college roommate did all my Christmas shopping, and a group of my daughter's thirteen-year-old friends fasted for me. The high school principal brings teachers, staff, and students to meet Brady. My married children's in-laws call and visit frequently, including us in all of their activities.

The children have seen firsthand what it means to truly care and to anticipate others' needs. How can they not feel loved? We are warned about being prideful, aren't we? It would be hard to be very proud when we are so needful. Bonds of love tighten when you look around and see what others have done for you. The act of service may be short lived, but the feelings of support and caring continue for a lifetime. We must be willing to admit when we need help and graciously accept it without ever expecting it. Every good deed should be replicated. That will be our family goal. It will take a lifetime to "get even."

Margaret Hafen Archibald

Margaret Archibald was born in St. George, Utah, in the days when it was a cozy little town of 5,000 and almost everybody knew everybody. When she was sixteen, her father, Orval, suddenly died of a heart attack, which changed her life forever. Her mother, Ruth, began teaching school and ended up teaching French at Dixie College for 21 years. Ruth passed away in 1995, after being a widow for 30 years and surviving the loss of two sons. Margaret feels that her mother taught her to love the gospel as well as the importance of patience, long-suffering, and a wonder for good music, fine art, great literature, and theater.

She met her husband, Nolan Archibald, when he came to Dixie College to play basketball. Even though he never made his high school team, he became an All-American and was recruited by 50 major colleges and universities. He chose to return to his home town of Ogden, Utah, and play at Weber State. Margaret managed to cram four years of class work into three years and also worked part-time during that third year, graduating with a degree in Elementary Education.

While Nolan earned an MBA from Harvard Business School, Margaret supported him by teaching school. They have moved around the country a number of times since then, literally from coast to coast. Nolan is president, CEO, and chairman of the Black and Decker Corporation, and he and Margaret have seven sons and one daughter. Margaret has served in almost every imaginable Church position, both teaching and leading in all the auxiliaries, and in several stake positions. She loves reading, traveling, playing tennis, cooking, and raising her family.

Looking Back

Viewing the relaxation therapy that occurs to mothers as they age

As my college-age boys come home now each spring to spend the summer at home, they are incredulous at what they see. I'll say to the 11-year-old, "Did you practice the piano yet today? Hurry and do it before you go to bed!" My 23-year-old (a 6'4" mass of manness) says, "What is going on here? What has happened since I grew up in this house?" He relays into shock again upon learning that bedtime for that 11-year-old is somewhere between 9:30 and 11:00. He commiserates with his brother-buddy (a 6'6" 24-year-old) and says, "Remember how it was for us? That alarm clock rang at 6:30 A.M. every morning with Mother standing in the doorway, military style, to make sure we made it to the piano bench and didn't stop playing until 7:10—not 7:09—but 7:10. Then and only then were we allowed to get ready for the day. And bedtime! If we weren't in bed by 8:00 P.M., every minute we were late was doubled and came off the next night's bedtime, making it even earlier than 8:00!" The shock continues as we eat our evening meal together. The 9-year-old only takes whatever she feels in the mood for, and if she's still hungry she fixes herself a bagel. But the real clincher came on a Friday evening when the 17-year-old announced his plans for the evening (not asking permission) and was told, "Don't come in too late."

So what has happened besides extreme fatigue from raising seven boys? We lightened up! Gradually over the years we realized that running a tight ship didn't mean being totally inflexible. I call it my "It All Comes Out in the Wash" theory, meaning that there are many different paths to take to the end of the road; as long as you're on the right road, it's less bumpy if you're more flexible, and you still end up with great kids.

Starting out as new parents, we wanted to teach obedience, discipline, good habits, and hard work. We tried so hard that we controlled every aspect of our child's life. With each individual child, we learned that some needed more structure than others. As they grew into the teen years, the decisions they made were more their own and they received the consequences. One of our boys decided he wanted to become the best athlete possible. He changed his eating habits, rejected all junk food, and asked for more fruits and vegetables. He made sure he got enough sleep. He reached his goal of having his body in the best condition, and he still follows those habits. I don't think it will be long until that nine-year-old makes the decision to try more healthy foods as she comprehends the impact of her current diet.

Coming home on weekend nights varies with the occasion. Midnight is a reasonable time to end activities. But if the video at the friend's house hasn't ended, or if someone needs a ride home, a phone call to the parents gives an approximate arrival time.

I remember when our first child was invited to a friend's Bar Mitzvah. It was to end around midnight. I embarrassed him by making him leave and come home at eleven because midnight was too late, in my mind, for an 11-year-old to be out. The next child came along and was invited to Bar Mitzvahs. I told him he could stay until midnight. But by the time boy number six started asking to go and told me it ended at 1:00 A.M., I surprised myself by just saying, "Can you get a ride home?" This certainly wasn't one of the character-forming life decisions.

Going with the flow of the circumstances made a lot more sense than preconceived set-in-stone rules.

How else have I lightened up? As I've lived through a few children from birth to young adulthood, I've realized that many, many of my little worries during each of their stages were totally unfounded. As an example, one of my boys was portraying undesirable traits as he hit age 11. I cornered my husband in desperation: "He's going to be a terrible marriage partner someday." My wise husband summed it up with, "That's why 11-year-olds don't get married." And he was right. That boy has grown into a wonderful young man. Each stage of development brings challenges and changes. But it's nice to know until those tumultuous teen years are over, it's just "work in progress."

Looking back, I see that my older boys may have been raised by uptight parents and the younger boys get the relaxed parents. The end result is a product from the same home with the same values and knowledge of what is really important in life. It's just much easier on parents and kids to have a more flexible perspective.

The Hard Times

A special ointment for life's daily struggles

The good thing about the hard times is that I hardly remember them. The magic phrase of "And this too shall pass" does pass difficult experiences into the corners of the mind where it takes some jiggling to recall them. At the time of the hardship, you think you'll never endure until it's over and you'll never forget what it felt like—just like giving birth to a child. But thankfully, life moves on.

I'm acutely aware that my hard times don't even come close to hard when compared with many others. But to me, they were my big problems and had to be overcome, requiring a search for resources to make it through.

My first hard time as a mother was that I couldn't become a mother. I assumed that after we finished college and started graduate school, those cute little babies would start coming. I was shocked that month after month went by with no signs of pregnancy. Being a mother was my planned "profession." I had majored in elementary education in college so I would have a good background to raise children. I had even minored in child development. I did teach school as I waited for my "real" profession to begin.

At first, I was frustrated that it was taking so long. After five years, panic set in. I went through several medical procedures and several doctors. I stopped going to friends' baby showers because it hurt too much. I braced myself when unknowing acquaintances would ask, "When are you going to

start your family?" Finally, after starting the adoption process, and after seeing a specialist and having an incredible
priesthood blessing, the miracle occurred! When that baby
was placed in my arms nine months later, I thought to myself, "Every single child that comes into this world should be
so desperately wanted and ached for." There certainly would
be more loved children, and motherhood would be a crowning
reward.

Ironically, with that first birth my medical problems were
solved, and every two years another boy would enter our family, which leads me to another of my "hard times." After seven
boys in fourteen years, I was in over my head. There were so
many days I thought, "What have I done?" My coping skills
had vanished, my patience level had reached zero; I even
questioned my sanity. Now I look at our old home movies and
wonder how I ever lived through it. It was especially difficult
during the long Chicago winters where October meant it was
time to come inside and good luck until the end of May. Boys
were not made to be housebound. It was also very difficult
every Sunday as I struggled through the years of pretending
I had things under control during sacrament meeting. How I
wished that ward and stake leaders thought my husband's
calling should be to help me on Sundays instead of serving in
positions that required him to not ever sit with me for fifteen
years. How I admired families whose children actually sat
without moving during the whole meeting. I remember one
fast Sunday I was unaware that the microphone for testimony
bearing was being passed down my row. As I reached for the
baby starting to crawl under the bench, I heard my two-year-
old and four-year-old in a tussle. With "end of my rope" frustration, as loudly as I could, I said "SHHHHHHHHH!!!" just
as my six-year-old passed the microphone in front of my lips.
The whole chapel heard my feelings. I also remember someone who actually said to me after one particularly grueling
Sunday, "You'd better get control or you'll never make it
when they are teenagers." Well, finally as teenagers, they

don't move at all during sacrament meeting. They may be asleep, but at least I get to listen to the meeting.

Adding to the challenge of a large family of boys was the fact that my husband traveled a lot; many times I felt like a single parent. My husband also thought it would be really fun and interesting to change jobs and move every two years. We did actually stay in one city four years. Talk about hard times! With every move came the painful goodbyes to good friends who had been such a great support system, and the pain of leaving familiar surroundings and comfort zones. Each new location brought months of adjusting and worrying about each child's emotional well-being. It was hard to start over each time with new schools, new friends, new highways—let alone finding new doctors and dentists and plumbers! The last move we made from Chicago to Washington, D.C., was the toughest. The older boys were old enough to find it impossible to sever the ties and face the unknown. I never saw my husband, who was very engrossed in his new job, besides his two-hour-and-twenty-minute round-trip commute. I also became pregnant with child number eight *and* remodeled the house we bought. How could my body betray me so cruelly by having insomnia now of all times? But we survived it all and have absolutely thrived!

You really can live through hard times. It sometimes takes lots of tears and even a brief "running away from home." I remember many times of reaching the "end of the rope" that was getting shorter with each progressive year and just running outside to the backyard to scream silently. Then I would take a deep breath, refocus my perspective, and say, "I can do this." It also helped to find a strong shoulder to cry on and to have lots of talks with a Heavenly Father who knew my troubles.

It's also interesting that these few "hard times" I've described have brought me my greatest joys in life. I wouldn't trade one of those exciting places where we lived nor one of the people we know. And the privilege of raising a large family has been worth every second of pain and agony. I am now seeing the fruits of my labors. The payoff is beyond what I imagined. There have been so many exquisite moments that cannot be matched by worldly honors. One of those moments was felt as we completed a temple session for our third son in preparation for his mission. What joy as I looked at these grown boys who were now my best friends. There will always be some form of hard times, but I'm glad they fade to the past.

"Don't You Have Any Ears?"

Rehabilitating for those who are always too busy to enjoy their children

The day I brought my seventh son home from the hospital was a Sunday in May—Mother's Day. It was a great way to celebrate an otherwise potentially depressing day. With the baby fed and sleeping, and my husband entertaining the six other energy-infused males, I glanced at the *Chicago Tribune* Sunday section, a special article on the joys of mothers and daughters. My heart returned to the frequent yearnings I had felt with each new pregnancy. "I'm sure *this* time it will be a girl!" As I once again returned the lacy, pink clothes and blankets to the department store, not wanting to tell the clerk the reason for the return, I resolved within that I was to be a mother of boys. That joyful bond between a mother and daughter would not be part of my experience. Anyway, I reminded myself, boys are much easier to raise—less complicated and less emotional.

Three years later, as I braced myself for boy number eight (the doctors had assured me), the delivery was so difficult that I just wanted that baby to finally come into the world, even if it was another boy. When the doctor announced, "It's a girl!" the shock was so great that it took me several seconds to realize what had been said. Then a flood of emotions filled that delivery room from laughter and squeals to tears and hysterical happiness.

Over the next few days, all I could do was smile. As I held

that precious new spirit in my arms and looked at the long, feminine fingers, I daydreamed about all the things I had repressed for twenty years—hair done up in bows; beautiful, frilly dresses; ballet shoes; even a wedding dress.

Then as I got home and settled into reality, my thoughts expanded to resolves of being a good mother. I thought, "This is my last chance to get this mothering thing right. Look at all my past experience and knowledge to help me." I wanted to make sure I took lots of pictures and put them immediately into albums, took lots of videos, and kept a journal of all milestones and cute sayings. I wanted to make sure she was introduced to the best children's books, which I would read nightly to her. But most of all, I wanted to give her lots of hugs and kisses with those bedtime stories and to be patient in all the phases of growing. I wanted her to feel how much I loved her.

I tried hard with these resolves, being a better mother to all eight children. But life was too real. I had to be reminded so many times.

One of those times was when my daughter was nearing the end of her "terrible twos." One night I was extra tired as I began the dreaded "time for bed" routine. After three times of my telling that little toddler that she *had* to go to bed, she ran off in another direction with just one more important task she had to get done. I raised my voice in total frustration, "Come back here now!" In fact, I fell to my knees in agony and exhaustion. Then that sweet, precious soul I had longed for came running back to me. She took her chubby little hands, the ones with the feminine fingers, put them around my face, and said, in a loud voice reflecting the tone she had just heard from me, "Don't you have any ears?" I was a little stunned, and it took me a moment to comprehend what she meant. If you can't hear very well, you think you have to yell to be heard. But isn't it better on ears to hear a softer, kinder voice? I have often thought about that lesson since my child taught it to me. There have also been times when I've seen a distraught mother scream at her child, a little person still learning the process of growing up, and I've wanted to calm her down and gently ask, "Don't you have any ears?"

It's so hard to consistently be the mother we wish we could be. But that doesn't mean we don't keep trying. We make a mistake, get back up, and head in the right direction.

I don't think my daughter will remember the lesson she taught me as much as I do. I think she's going to remember the feelings she felt when I held her close as we read those books and looked at the photos of her life. She will also remember that I said I was sorry when I made those inevitable mistakes. I hope she remembers the times we played together, down on the floor with puzzles and games, or the bike rides or nature walks. I finally learned to say no to many of the distractions that kept me from having time for her. Listening with the ears my daughter taught me to have, I sensed that I had to pull away from my hectic life and really identify the most important time consumers. I found myself missing unimportant meetings, not signing up for the class Valentine party, and even buying birthday cakes from the bakery instead of making my four-hour creations. I cut down on the number of endless lessons and activities that pulled me away from home. I knew the years would whizz by, and I had to grab my chances. That mother and daughter bond I wanted so much would only happen by our spending lots of time together, even if I had to be reminded to be more patient.

The Next Profession

Remembering to appreciate the pain relievers of the Church and the temporary pains of motherhood

My husband and I were talking recently about the new stage of parenting that is coming next for us—the empty nest. I told him that it was time for me to start pursuing my next profession—to get a job in the real world like he has. I was surprised by his response. He said, "Nothing is as rewarding and fulfilling as raising a family—not even my job." Here is the CEO of a major corporation who absolutely loves what he does. He's also been able to be very involved with the family, so he does know how rewarding it is to watch a child grow and develop into a wonderful adult.

As I look back on my mothering profession, I've realized how lucky I am to be able to be a stay-at-home mother. The early years were very challenging as I felt isolated and tried to keep intellectually stimulated. But isolation turned to massive interaction as I changed from a mother at home to a mother in a car.

I also appreciated being a member of The Church of Jesus Christ of Latter-day Saints. I have raised my family in "the mission field," and I feel that experience has made me appreciate what the Church gives me. Sometimes I've had non-member friends congratulate me on what wonderful, terrific kids I have. I naturally want to take credit, but I realize the outstanding qualities they possess that set them apart from the rest of the world come because Jesus Christ has been their greatest influence. I wonder if these complimentary friends have seen a pattern of sacrifice and high standards that provided the results they see.

These friends are astonished when they hear about my teenagers getting up at 5:30 A.M. every weekday morning for religious instruction, as well as giving up one night a week for an activity and devoting all of Sunday to their religion and family. They have been very aware of no sports played on Sunday. One coach even got a Sunday playoff game changed so he'd have a better chance of winning. Another coach wrote our son a letter of praise for sticking to his standards, and this was after the team lost the Sunday championship game by one point. Our friends admire our trust that we don't have to worry about drinking and drugs. Many of the starters on the lacrosse team had to miss the championship game for breaking the drinking rule, except for my two boys. They were very instrumental in the win. Going on a mission is another impressive sacrifice. And what a difference in the young man who returns after serving Jesus Christ for two years versus his classmates and what they've been doing in those twenty-four months!

I'm so glad I had the knowledge that, as a mother at home with her children, I was doing the most important work in the world. I had lots of help along the way. The Church offers such a strong support system with organizations and role models. That should never be taken for granted. And to be led by a living prophet gives such a sense of security in a floundering world.

With this religious conviction and faith, I see how much prayer has meant in my mothering role. Those answers to my earnest prayers were not always immediate or complete, but they came. And they came in ways I didn't recognize at first. When I was struggling with different aspects of motherhood, a friend or an experience would give me the answers.

I learned immensely from other mothers. Just watching and talking showed me the way. I also learned from my own mother and mother-in-law.

I learned from my mother-in-law whenever she would come for a visit. My children loved to be around her because she showed so much love and patience. She would get right down on the floor and just play, whether it was a two-year-old with toys or a seven-year-old with a game.

I learned much from my own mother, who was my beacon of light through the years with our weekly long-distance phone calls. Two conversations stand out in my memory. One was when she sensed my discouragement and reminded me to make sure I was not neglecting the four necessary areas of a stress-free life—emotional (thank goodness for friends), physical (which I was definitely neglecting), spiritual (of course I should be able to read at least one page in the Book of Mormon before my day starts or before I go to bed), and intellectual (another void).

The other crucial advice came after my mother heard my overwhelming burdens: "It sounds like you need to give some service to someone else." It was amazing what happened when I turned my thoughts and actions towards other people. That always lifted my spirits.

I'm grateful also that my knowledge has made me appreciate that motherhood is a partnership with God. He entrusts his spirits to my care and training. What a sacred duty and obligation!

I can see that being a parent is the best environment to learn Christlike qualities. In trying to do our best as mothers and fathers, we are developing traits that make us better people. We grow by leaps and bounds every time we strive for patience, kindness, love, service, humility, and being in tune with the Spirit. It's a very difficult and long process that takes a lot of trial and error along the way, but the rewards are not measured in earthly terms. The time and effort my husband and I have put into raising our children in the gospel have given more satisfaction than anything else we've done. If I decide to do my next profession, I'll be prepared to find the rewards a little different, but I'll also know my motherhood profession is the one that has made me into a better person.

The Sheep and the Wolves

Administering antibiotics for raising children
in the mission field

I hesitate to enter this subject since I'm still floundering as I go. With the way the world is today and with the area where I live, I sometimes feel as I watch my children leave my home each day that they are vulnerable sheep being thrown to a den of wolves with very few survival tactics. Maybe I'm not alone in my anxieties as I look at the evil, wicked environment we live in and wonder if it could get any worse. I feel totally outnumbered as I try to teach my children to battle the big Goliath. As in many other mothering skills, I stumble as I go and wonder how to do it.

My daughter goes to a school where she is the only member of the LDS Church. What a challenge she has ahead of her! My boys attend a school where there are only three or four other families who identify with their background and standards.

Most of the kids in these schools start drinking at the age of sixteen, with parties every weekend throughout their years in high school. This is just a normal phase of growing up for them. My children find it impossible to have close friends all week and then not be able to see those friends on the weekends. This is a constant battle that we continue to deal with because these friends are basically terrific kids who have a totally different view on life.

I also live in an area where there are ten different high

schools represented in our small ward. It's very unfortunate, because I know of numerous wards along the East Coast where the LDS teenagers band together and have an incredibly good time all through their high school years. They are creative and consistently have something fun planned every weekend. Even their non-LDS friends join in the fun and are surprised by the good time they have.

With television, radio, and movies being taken over by evil forces, I just hope I have taught my children the necessary coping skills.

The most important strength of power comes from the beginning stages of a personal testimony. With faith that the gospel is true, hopefully our children will make good choices. And that foundation comes from being taught as early as possible by example and family scripture study and family home evening. Doing lots of activities together as a family also is a source of strength and a help in building a testimony.

The next piece of armor in this battle would be a good relationship with Mom and Dad. My husband told me he never thought of doing anything wrong as a teenager because he would never want to hurt his mom and dad. And having a good relationship, you're able to openly communicate about ways you can help save them from the evil forces.

Sometimes as parents we have to gently steer when we see a potential danger in friends that may be damaging or lead to questionable environments. I had to smile when my seventeen-year-old son saw my husband and me all dressed up to go to the company Christmas party. He said, "Will there be drinking there?" We said, "Yes." He said, "I don't feel good about you going." I was glad he had been listening to our advice and wanted to give it to us.

I've had my grown children thank me now for stopping them from heading in a wrong direction with friends who weren't good for them. It was very reassuring when one son on a mission was talking to his teenage brother one Christmas day on the telephone and said, "Make sure you listen to

Mom and Dad. I hate to admit it, but they're always right."
Well, maybe not *always*, but at least our kids know we love
them so much that we are always watching out for their eternal happiness.

Raising a family in an area where being LDS is in the mi-
nority can be challenging and yet an advantage. My older
sons tell me how great it was to already be different in those
teenage years where kids are struggling for an identity. And
all their friends knew their unusual standards, admired
them for keeping them, and would have been extremely disappointed if they ever slipped.

My greatest hope as I get these "sheep" raised is to make
sure their coping skills are strong enough to not be harmed
by the "wolves." I also hope they find strength with their
other LDS friends, though they may be few in number, and
together provide a great example to others.

Memories

Applying a hot pack to warm
your happy memories

Some recent experiences have made me think a lot about memories lately. Last fall, I lost my elderly mother. I knew it was coming for quite a few years and kept trying to prepare myself to let her go. But she was such a vital part of my life, such a connection to who I was, that I couldn't imagine life without her. I guess I'll never stop thinking about her and missing her, so I'll hold on to the memories and teachings and hope the empty feeling gets smaller. At her funeral, I reflected on her full and varied life, one that was devoted to being a mother. I was grateful to have been the recipient of that love and nurturing.

Then last May I heard one of my friends give a tribute to her deceased mother in a sacrament meeting talk on Mother's Day. She beautifully gave details of her mother's attributes. She talked about her cheerfulness, optimism, generosity, selflessness, sense of humor, acceptance of responsibility, hard work, love for all around her, trust, and nurturing. How I wish my children, in thinking of me, will remember even a few such qualities!

Then I read an article in the *Washington Magazine,* a publication to remind me of the real world that I'm surrounded by. The timely article was called "The Nanny Generation" and discussed kids of the 70s and 80s who were raised by nannies and how their lives were affected. It was very interesting since I live in an area where most households have live-in help so the mothers can pursue a career. I found it intriguing that the childhood memories were very similar to children raised by mothers at home. What would my children say if they were asked for their memories?

One of the young adults interviewed about her nanny remembers with fondness a panda bear cake made for a birthday party. Another one remembers getting macaroni and cheese whenever asked. Other fond memories were stories at bedtime and help given with building a fort out of umbrellas. The nannies they liked the best showed a "bounty of love, were positive role models and plain old fun."

One sixteen-year-old chose to discuss her boyfriend with her nanny because she didn't feel she could talk to her mom. She perceived her mom as overprotective, whereas her nanny had an easygoing attitude that made for a happy environment for children.

One girl didn't have fond memories of one of her nannies. She remembers getting spanked for peeling the paper off crayons and putting baking soda on construction paper.

A good nanny was remembered as being fair, nurturing, warm, committed to family and values. They were also remembered as fun to hang out with. One made wonderful lemonade, went for walks with the child, and just talked with her.

A moment as insignificant as a nanny laughing at a child's joke and later telling his mom caused one child to feel loved and believe in his sense of humor. This same child also remembers that when he was in the third grade and started reading science books, the nanny told his mom how special he was. He felt a rise in his self-esteem. A more negative memory was offered by a girl who felt loved until her sister was born; then she felt completely unimportant and in the way.

Some of the working moms went out of their way to do something special with each child. These children felt *they* were their parents' priority.

When asked what would improve their happiness and home life, the kids chose spending more time with parents and enjoying more open communication with them. Fathers especially had a positive influence spending time with their children, being involved and nurturing.

We can't control our children's memories or their interpretation of events. But by keeping in mind that we only get to raise them once, we ought to provide a relaxed, loving atmosphere where our children feel they are our top priority by the little things we do for them and by the amount of time we spend together. And if strong memories come from children and their nannies, just think how much more powerful those memories would be from sharing experiences with parents, the ones who love them and know them more than anyone else they come in contact with.

Maybe many years from now I'll have a child with good memories, one who pays tribute to my mothering efforts, or even one who misses our being together.

Ann Whiting Orton

Ann Whiting Orton grew up on a farm in Mapleton, Utah, as the oldest of four children. She graduated from BYU with both bachelor's and master's degrees. Married and divorced, she has raised six children.

Most of her time has been spent mothering independently since, even before her divorce, her first husband's job required extensive travel. In addition to her full life as a mother, she has been employed as a high school teacher, preschool teacher, and food editor for the Salt Lake City *Deseret News*.

In 1992 she married Russell B. Orton. Recently, after six years of working full time, Ann was apprehensive to return home with her children mostly grown but has poured her talents into other causes and enjoys her independence. She has also found great joy in Russell's insight and support with her children. She deems it one of her greatest blessings to always be able to rely on the priesthood for sustenance. Currently Ann is fulfilling a lifelong dream to design and build a new home. In fact, one of life's biggest treasures for her is realizing that sometimes dreams do come true.

The Call

Presenting a balm for those who have lost a child

Interviews. A physical examination. Forms and signatures. Ninety days. White envelopes. Temple endowments. Farewells. Missionary Training Center. Airlines. Letters from field.

The countdown begins as young men approach their nineteenth year of age and anticipate service as full-time missionaries. Years of preparation, goal setting, saving, and experience culminate in the opportunity to open the bulging envelope that directs their missionary term of service to a geographic assignment.

A mission call looms as a rite of passage to young priesthood holders and to many of their dedicated sister missionary counterparts. It is a cycle of service ongoing in the Church since the early days—a commandment of a prophet, a family expectation, and a remarkable blessing to all.

Mission calls usually come in a timely manner and under the inspiration and signature of the living prophet. Some mission calls, however, differ. I waited almost nine months for Benjamin to receive his call. Nothing routine about his eternal assignment to teach the gospel. And now, as his earthly age approaches nineteen, I ponder the possibilities of his lifetime mission.

There was no white envelope for Ben, no interview, no temple experience, and no training at the MTC. He came prepared to serve almost immediately. The Lord called him home

to begin his missionary efforts when he'd had only nine brief
months of earthly preparation. His physical body failed to sit,
stand, or walk, but his spiritual being was ready to serve.

Ben was the fifth of my children and the fourth son. He
was the only comfortable pregnancy I had—a sleepy baby
that was so considerate of his mother. Never did he hang his
tiny feet at some awkward angle on my rib cage; his hiccups
were rhythmic and gentle. Even with four others at home, including two preschoolers, I was convinced I could carry this
baby for twelve months, maybe even fifteen. When he finally
made his scheduled appearance, I discovered the answer.
Ben was a floppy baby, more like Raggedy Andy than G.I.
Joe. All the better to cuddle, I assumed.

Then the doctors began analyzing Ben's snuggly little
body. One by one they posed questions, ran tests, and raised
more questions.

There were no immediate answers to the medical questions.

I began asking the Lord a few questions of my own. I
longed to know what Benjamin's physical limitations would
mean to our family life. I begged to understand why I had
been given this challenge. Most of all, I pleaded to understand how I could help solve Ben's problems.

My daily routines evolved to include hours of medical
tests, doctor's consultations, physical therapy sessions inter-
rupted by car pools, Church callings, and unyielding stacks
of laundry.

After six weeks of examinations, genetic testing, and
counseling, I packed our five children on an airplane and
flew home to the summer peace of the mountains and family.
We spent a month gathering strength and family support
while Little Ben struggled to swallow. Nursing him took a
full hour per feeding, but supplementing with a bottle overwhelmed his swallow reflex and he choked.

At last my daily experience in caring for him uncovered
an answer. He couldn't swallow effectively. Armed with my
discovery, I returned to my pediatrician's office with the solu-

tion—my "fix" for Ben's difficulties. Dr. Hogan noted my observations but failed to share my enthusiasm. Only days after our visit, Ben came down with pneumonia and required two weeks' hospitalization.

It was then that my family away from the mountains, the Indianapolis Fifth Ward, began their months of service to our family. Jared, two, moved in with our home teachers, the Dodsons (who graciously toilet trained him while he was there). Amy, four, stayed with the Wilsons a block away. Greg, nine, and Jeff, seven, worked their school schedules around the hospital and parental work requirements but received uncounted dinners and treats.

My hospital hours were sustained by my obstetrician, Joe Plautz, who intervened with the attending physicians whenever my emotions crumbled.

Ben arrived home briefly, only to return to the hospital with a recurrence of pneumonia several weeks later. A third hospitalization finally revealed the information I had previously suggested. Ben had trouble swallowing; his intake aspirated to his lungs and created the infection. He was surgically fitted with a gastrostomy, or "tummy tube," so we could feed him directly into his stomach.

Nurses became our second family, the hospital our second home. Christmas 1977 evolved into an isolation hospital stay when Ben responded to his surgical medications with congestive heart failure. His brief stay at home resulted in exposure to the chicken pox—two cases—and he couldn't share those bumps with his hospital friends.

Six months with Ben and I'd settled into a frantic routine of basic survival. Ina Duerden, a nurse in the ward, came weekly to tend him so I could get groceries, run errands, and even sit quietly at the library. Just a few hours alone fortified my ability to return to the demands of the family.

Seven months. Eight months and counting. Still no definitive answers, still a very ill infant with but minute signs of progress. Ben gradually responded to the hours of physical therapy and even gained weight. His final clinic visits yielded high marks from each of his doctors and a gentle head raise and smile for the physical therapist—and for me. Optimistic for a long-term prognosis, we returned home.

The next morning Benjamin received his call, a quiet summons to come home to the labors of a new life.

There was no envelope to announce a field of labor and a departure date. Nothing but a stilled form barely gasping for breath. *How could this be?* I questioned. The previous day's reports had been so encouraging, yet I knew something was dreadfully wrong. Fire station, resuscitation, emergency room, ambulance, intensive care, life support, and a priesthood blessing. I only saw Ben once during the final hours of his struggle. It was then I received the assurance that his mortal experience was complete and that I could let him return home to his Heavenly Father.

Grief was a lonely process, a step-by-step, day-by-day longing for peace. To understand Benjamin's earthly mission required faith through study and prayer and mountains of work on my part—both with Ben and with the medical personnel. Sharing his lifetime also necessitated receiving help from many other people, an acknowledgment that the Lord answered my pleas through the generous service of others. Most of all, dealing with my infant son's premature mission call provided an opportunity to experience the influence of the Holy Ghost in new and varied dimensions. At times I felt complete comfort, almost like being wrapped in a cozy blanket; at other times I struggled for peace. Only when I faced gnawing feelings of desperation did the peace return. I discovered that workings of the Spirit are somewhat cyclical: when I was strong, the Spirit rested; as I crumbled, spiritual support packaged my soul. As time passed, I noticed the transfusions of spiritual strength enabled me to function for longer periods of time before the emotional floodgates burst. When discouragement returned, I was again and again buoyed up.

Years later, as weekly mission reports arrived at our home, I longed for a heavenly message from Benjamin. What experiences has his 19-year mission included? Could I compare the teaching opportunities, the joys of baptism, the discouragement of closed doors, and the satisfaction of diligent service to the earthly missions served in Japan, Hong Kong, and Montreal? I pray that Ben reported detailed entries in a journal describing his missionary labors, a daily summary of his growth in testimony.

More than that, I pray that when my final call arrives, I will be worthy to share in the accomplishments and lessons of his eternal missionary experience. Then I will study and learn from the letters he recorded as he served the eternal term of his mission call.

Just Fine, Thank You

Introducing psychotherapy for the frozen-
smile-even-though-you're-dying syndrome

Only one errand to do on Friday—please, Mom, find me a book at the library, my oldest daughter requested as she raced out the door for class. Not that challenging, I reasoned. I could drive to the library and check out a book in my present condition. A few controlled minutes in public seemed possible, but I'd keep the tissue box close by in case another unsuspected event triggered an untimely flow of tears.

I drove to the city library, delighted to find two adjacent parallel parking spaces. After parking the car without incident, I began the search for the book. The card catalog announced the classification numbers, even the floor location, so I ambled along to the escalator. No tissues required as yet. Once in the stacks, I began the search for the title. I looked for five minutes, counting number to number in vain. I was in the correct spot; why was the book missing? Without warning, the flood of frustration set off the tears and I began to cry. Before long I was crying uncontrollably, sobbing and searching for a tissue, not a title. Finally my wailing attracted the attention of a library employee who came to my rescue. She ushered me into the restroom and tried to uncover the source of my dismay. I gave her the standard Mormon mom reply—"I'm just fine"—as I endeavored to regain my composure. Reassured that I wasn't immediately suicidal, she left me to my puddles and swelling eyes.

Why was I crying? What caused me to lose control of my emotions over such a simple thing as a missing book? Another episode like this, I reasoned, and I'd be locked up. In fact, I considered driving myself directly to the emergency room for assistance. But a brief reality check reminded me that Emily, my grade school daughter, would be home shortly and be locked out of the house if I weren't there. I left the library empty-handed and red-eyed, found my car, and drove back home without the book. I had failed one more time.

The library encounter was only one of many emotional collapses following the departure of my husband of 22 years. After several years in a roller coaster relationship, he left for the final time. We had recently relocated to Salt Lake City after a five-year assignment in North Carolina. We moved into our new home and went through all the motions of being a healthy, functional family. We even managed to present our family "welcome to the ward" introductions in sacrament meeting.

On the Sunday after we spoke in church, I sat alone on the pews and cried through the meetings. A concerned sister approached me after a drippy hour and asked if she could help. I dabbed at my eyes and explained that I was "just fine," and she moved on through the crowd. Much to my surprise, she called later in the day to check again. Then she called every day with a message of concern and support. I dutifully persisted that I was "just fine," not yet ready to unburden my real concerns on a stranger.

After the library scene, I recognized that "just fine" was blatantly inaccurate. I was immersed in emotional turmoil, and I had no idea how to begin the climb out. I finally called my neighbor and told her my husband had left us. She came over, but not before she'd called her physician husband and arranged a counseling appointment for me. Carol took care of Emily, my grade school daughter, left a note for the other children, then drove me to the doctor's offices. She waited for me during the session, then drove me home once again, a procedure she continued throughout the following week. As the long days turned into weeks, my supportive and loving neighbor continued to share time and energy with me.

I finally admitted that only complete desperation had motivated me to call Carol after the library collapse. After all, I reasoned, I was an educated and capable woman. I lived the commandments, attended my meetings, served in the ward, studied my scriptures, and said my prayers. I thought I'd done what I should do to solve the problems I was facing, but I was sinking lower and lower. I recognized that a solution to my problems was beyond my individual resources. Even my pleadings with the Lord often seemed unheard, but it was I who couldn't comprehend the answers he sent.

In my struggles, I consistently overlooked a basic premise of the gospel taught by the Savior: service to our brothers and sisters is synonymous with service to our Heavenly Father (see Matthew 25:35–45). Rendering service to those in need constructs the underpinnings of a ward family unit. Oh, I knew this principle from years of service to others, but what I failed to understand was the significance of the principle in reverse. Service to our Heavenly Father is two-dimensional: we give *and* we receive. I'd spent my service hours in giving; I'd had only limited experience at the receiving end of the service spectrum.

Like thousands of Mormon sisters, I immediately responded to the beck and call of a Laurel girl, never considering my personal inconvenience. If one of my Young Women had a request, they knew I would help at a moment's notice. When my calling changed, the Relief Society sisters found the same reassurance. Dinners taken out the front door, children attended, illness watched over, and even a sister dressed for her casket became almost second nature as the variety of needs arose. Though others' needs were not always timely, I sensed the responsibility and offered assistance. We're schooled as mothers and sisters in the gospel to respond to the concerns of our neighboring brothers and sisters.

The second dimension of service seemed considerably less familiar. I'd caught glimpses of it when the babies arrived or when I moved into a new ward. When I had a baby with a long-term illness, many people offered support and energy. Otherwise, I considered myself independent, even self-sufficient, or even possibly proud.

Through the remarks of President Spencer W. Kimball, I eventually caught a glimpse of service as it should be from both sides. President Kimball suggested at a conference in 1974 that "God does notice us, and he watches over us. But it is usually through another mortal that he meets our needs. Therefore, it is vital that we serve each other in the kingdom." The principle glares with simplicity—we serve, but others must also serve us so the Lord is able to meet our needs.

Over time I have learned that the Lord truly answered my prayers according to his methods. He provided brothers and sisters from my own circle of contacts to help me over the hurdles of single mothering. It wasn't easy to accept the help, even after I gained an understanding of the process. I often struggled with pride and slipped into the standard "just fine" response. But eventually the weight of my concerns produced ample humility and I sought help again and again.

As the holidays approached in the first season alone, I anticipated traditional family events with no husband. Before I had an opportunity to mourn the lost traditional celebrations, others issued invitations. My bishop's family invited us for Christmas Eve supper and activities. My own family filled in every gaping calendar hole with togetherness. Timely deliveries of food nearly eliminated my need to cook for several weeks. We received generous offerings of service, and we survived our first Christmas alone.

After the New Year, I went to work. Exhausted by the new demands on my time and the continued emotional pressures, I was relieved to discover occasional neighborly deliveries on my porch when I arrived home from the office. Often the shared foods arrived anonymously. One sister delivered a loaf of homemade bread weekly for several weeks. I discovered later, through the watchfulness of another neighbor, that the tasty loaves were placed by a sister in an adjoining ward, a sister I'd never met. Such offerings delivered an unspoken message of love in a casserole, bread tin, or cookie jar.

Others delivered offerings of time to listen and encourage.

Late one January night, I awakened, terrified by a frightening dream. In my mind, I was convinced it was the end for me. I could see no alternative but to remove the weight of the problems I faced and take my own life. Despair pushed me to the prescription bottle on my nightstand. With the pill bottle in hand, I began to cry. Nothing logical came to mind, only a flurry of disjointed thoughts. Finally I reached for the telephone and called my neighbor. At 1:00 A.M., I opened the door to a warm embrace. Nyla listened as my disconnected thoughts emerged, then she reassuringly hugged me through my sobs. She stayed with me until the sun rose on a new day, a day that I could face because of Nyla's counsel.

Counsel from priesthood leaders assisted me in many circumstances, but particularly regarding my 12-year-old son. Jared, a newly ordained deacon, was called to home teach and was assigned to a dedicated companion, Bill England. Though he wasn't technically old enough for the calling, our bishop sensed a need to pair this questioning deacon with a dependable priesthood friend.

When difficult hours arose, Jared discovered companionship and support in the home of a family friend, Skip Brooks. Skip miraculously stepped into our lives and generously offered time and counsel to Jared and to me. Only a phone call away, he became a liaison who sustained my son through tempestuous adolescent years. I learned how to call Skip and admit that our situation was askew—that not everything was "just fine."

Home teachers provided vital service to our family, even though our outward impressions continued in the "just fine" mode. The Lord knew that despite our public appearances, our family required diligent support. I learned how to express my legitimate needs to priesthood leaders, then finally admitted dependence on others to help.

Allowing others to serve me and my family presented a difficult challenge. When I was involved in the divorce process, my needs were glaringly apparent. If I was to keep myself and my children committed to the gospel, I needed to exercise every possible resource. Reluctantly, I humbled myself to receive help from many outside sources. I finally announced that a circumstance was trying, that I didn't know how I'd manage until the next day. I knew my neighbors observed my obvious frustrations, and certainly the Lord gained an awareness of my troubles. Why keep pretending with a cheerful yet dishonest veneer?

Awkwardness accompanied my reception of help, but finally grew to understand the cycle of service. My time of neediness would ultimately be replaced with renewed opportunities to give diligent service again. Now I watch for the mothers who routinely describe their circumstances as "just fine." I sneak underneath the phrase to examine the weariness of attitude, determine how I might help, and render a simple act of service.

You see, I'm on the giving side of the cycle for today. I need to stockpile my reserves because I never know when the service cycle will roll me back to a receiving space. I only know that time will come once more—maybe I will have eliminated "just fine" from my vocabulary by then.

Meat Market Madness

Revealing realizations if you're feeling
sick about dating again

Parent conferences ran well beyond the designated schedule, forcing me to pick up the recipe-testing groceries much later than I had planned. A quick stop at the market yielded a hastily assembled collection of ingredients, then I stopped to pick out a cut of meat. A tall and distinguished-looking man on the opposite side of the meat counter asked if I could help him select a roast. My mind was racing through the remaining events of the evening, and I didn't want to be bothered with meat-cooking instructions. Almost shyly, he continued, "Well, you see, I'm single, and I'd really appreciate your advice." Feeling a sense of professional responsibility creep into my voice, I laughed and said, "Well, okay, it's part of my job," then gave him a pair of suggestions. He asked two more questions and then walked to the checkout counter with his purchases.

I did the same. As I drove home, I thought a second time about the encounter. I'd noticed the man earlier as he passed me going to the rear of the store with two pots of mums in his arms. I recalled how silly that looked and wondered why he didn't have a cart—he certainly couldn't select any more purchases encumbered as he was. When he returned to my vicinity, he had set the pots on the floor and began the conversation.

I still didn't get it. I was forty-something, newly divorced, and oblivious to the possibilities of renewing a male-female relationship. I was so engrossed in survival-one-more-day strategies that I completely missed an overture to friendship. When the telephone rang a week or so later, a male voice identified himself as the man from the meat market. (This is a true story.) I was totally unaware that my comments about my job had given him enough information to find my name and eventually my telephone number at work.

Now I had a dilemma—I'd been invited out to supper. It was a request for a date, an odd and completely unfamiliar notion to me. In some ways, I felt like I was 16 or 18 years old again. I remember laughing, even giggling, then trying to stifle the explosion of emotions welling up inside me. I considered myself mature, if not emotionally secure, during this divorce adjustment period.

Of course, I said no way, how ridiculous, are you joking? You see, I was a mother, a food writer, and a Primary teacher, and I had other more important things to do with my time. I was not some crazy college girl with marriage on my mind, or even an anxious middle-aged socialite. I carried a divorce label that Band-aided all sorts of relationship issues. With that bandage of protection, my social life was clearly defined—I attended ward parties with my children and occasionally joined married friends when an extra ticket or reservation became available. I'd already learned how to play it safe in my new world.

The gentleman called again, apparently unfazed by my insistent refusal. This time the request was lunch, a luncheon near the office so I could get back to work right away. I paused in my cautious analysis—not quite so frightened by this closed-end social engagement. He sensed my momentary change of heart, then I panicked and refused a second time. This time a tiny spark of curiosity motivated me to launch an investigation of the "meat man." I'd gathered enough information to link his life to others I knew, so I requested a "credibility report" from mutual acquaintances. He passed the inspection process.

After his third call, I finally agreed to meet him for supper at a nearby restaurant. I drove my own car so escape would be readily available if necessary. Much to my surprise, I had a delightful conversation, a free meal, and another invitation. Dating wasn't as uncomfortable as I remembered, but I cautioned myself not to get overly enthused about the process.

That first date was one of many over the five years I was single, but it was the only date I ever had that was not arranged by friends. I became a line-up pro, trusting others to screen and recommend those whom I dated. It was safer that way, I convinced myself. No trips to the much-maligned singles' dance "meat market" for me. I drew a boundary that protected my fragile emotional state; then I lived within its thin walls.

As the months passed, my desire to reestablish an eternal companionship increased. I'd learned many lessons in single parenting and recognized that the Lord had much more for me to experience in my lifetime. Cautiously, I followed the timely advice of the "meat market" man. He once described a scenario that seemed tailored for my inhibitions. "If you walk along the edge of the ocean," he explained, "you can exercise as you view the vast expanse of sea ahead—and you are safe. If you step into the water, you may contact a jellyfish, a surprising shift in the sands or a stiff current, but you will probably remain upright and safely return to the shore. If, on the other hand, you dive head first into the water and swim out a mile or two, you discover the enchantment of the sea: scratchy residue of salt water, the ebb and flow of the waves and the buoyancy of your body as you conform to the currents. Of course, you take the chance of losing control and succumbing to the powers of the ocean, but you also discover the opportunity to explore uncharted territory before you swim back to the security of the shore.

"It's your choice," he concluded.

So it is with relationships: the safety of a continued walk on the shore eliminates the opportunity to experience the multiple sensory dimensions of an ocean swim. Still, from my perspective, prudence prevailed. I was first willing to only wade cautiously into a relationship, then I took a quarter-mile swim before I retreated to the shore for protection.

I discovered second-time-around dating to be cyclical, depending on my emotional courage at a given time. I often prayed for United Parcel to deliver the man of my dreams on my doorstep, a delivery in response to my carefully considered order specifications. Of course, the Lord suggested that I assume a greater responsibility myself to uncover workable new circumstances for me and for my children.

Oh, the children! Not only had I prayed for companionship for me but also for the kids. Adding kids to the dating equation creates untold concerns.

I recall a night I received a fresh Maine lobster delivery as a part of my job as a food editor. The package contained *everything* needed for the feast—even the pot to boil the lobster. After it arrived I set about preparations, which took on three children and a man I had been dating regularly. The kids reluctantly participated, but soon displayed their frustrations by bickering at the table, whining about the lobster as a menu item, then initiating a food fight that culminated in the 13-year-old son chasing his 9-year-old sister around the table with a lobster claw. Emily screamed in fright, escaped to her room, and sobbed. So much for a cheerful family activity.

Awkward encounters continued between the children and my male friends. The children were generally indifferent to my dates, often ignoring them to a point of rudeness. My 16-year-old daughter expressed occasional frustrations that her mother had a date when she didn't. My son's friends arrived one evening as I was involved in a doorstep embrace, embarrassing all of us. My younger daughter, concerned about a telephone disagreement I had with a friend, once sneaked out of our house and walked about three miles to his house in an attempt to resolve my problem.

After a period of time, some men extended friendship to

the children. I encouraged this building process in my early dating years, but then realized I must establish a positive relationship first and the family contacts would comfortably occur or not as time passed. In general, the kids found it uncomfortable to admit their mother had a "boyfriend." Their emotions were also in a state of upheaval, inspiring them to select the safety of the shore, to not be involved, rather than to swim the unpredictable turbulence of the ocean waves. They too had questions of trust to resolve.

Despite the awkward and cautious communications between the children and my friends, I longed to find someone who would fit comfortably into our previously established family circle. A companion for me was also a stepfather for my children. Obvious as it appears, both sets of needs were difficult to appease simultaneously. When I found someone I thoroughly enjoyed spending time with, I felt obligated to observe his interactions and attitudes toward the children. When my personal relationship was stimulating and exciting, his relationship with the children was often limited.

Other factors then determined my relationship choices as my confidence grew: a commitment to the gospel as a way of life, ease of communication, financial stability, and a sense of responsibility overrode my personal whims or romantic fantasies.

Eventual possibilities of romance brought another issue to the forefront: what was the appropriate way to define a physical relationship with a date? An insightful and formerly divorced neighbor man suggested an analogy that described my frustrations in this area. He compared the development of a physical relationship to a speedometer: for never-married singles the odometer reading registered 0–20 miles per hour, over an hour's time. In contrast, previously married folks often traveled 0–100 miles per hour in about 10 seconds. For me, it was a visual representation of how quickly a physical relationship could become intimate for the formerly married, information that required a thoughtful decision on my part.

Another part of the physical relationship dilemma involved the children. When was physical contact appropriate in their presence? Even a simple hug or impulsive kiss on the cheek sent a message of concern or embarrassment to the children, yet the kids needed to be aware of natural expressions of affection between people who care about each other. Obviously, such a decision required a response based on individual circumstances, personal comfort zones, and the commitment level of a particular relationship. For me, a casual approach finally prevailed. I kept distance between dates and children after several long-term relationships dissolved. The emotional upheaval affected the children as it affected me—we were found swimming in wind-swollen waves and retreated to the safety of the shore.

Children-and-dating concerns reversed themselves when I dated a man with children of his own. Similar experiences and feelings happened to me as the outsider, enabling me to more fully understand the complications and questions my own children faced. The shoe, or the swim fin, fit equally awkwardly on either side of the relationship and required conscientious attention and a definition of limits.

After five years of assorted dating adventures and swimming lessons, I received a call from a 78-year-old friend of mine who invited me to dinner with a friend of hers. As a matter of courtesy and with a touch of curiosity, I went. Sister Durham made all the arrangements so we would be properly introduced, including calling me from the car phone when the two of them arrived to pick me up. The gentleman got out of the car, introduced himself, and then opened the back door for me to climb in. My matchmaker friend spent most of the evening citing reasons for us to marry, regardless of the fact that we had only met minutes before. It was an embarrassing evening for both of us, so I was surprised when Russell invited me to dinner a second time—without Sister Durham. After 15 months, Russell and I were married in the Salt Lake Temple, sealed for time and all eternity.

I'm blessed with a happy beginning story to alter my singleness: a wonderful, romantic encounter to complete my telephone order to United Parcel Service. It wasn't as simple as placing an order by telephone, but when the right circumstance appeared in my life, I was almost ready. A long courtship included a variety of interactions, including a major surgery and subsequent eight-week recovery period for my younger daughter. I observed Russ in many situations with our family before I made a commitment. Once he asked and I agreed, then I panicked again. I'd said yes, but doubts crept in and trust issues surfaced. I finally said yes a second time, then got sick. I was diagnosed with some weird virus that zapped my energy supply. I wondered if my illness was a message that I'd made an incorrect decision. But the positive feelings prevailed, and Russ and I finally married. I was once again on the path our Heavenly Father intended for me and for my children.

During my years of longing for companionship, I searched for a shortcut to the desired result. I wanted to swim out to a distant island of paradise before I learned to doggy paddle. My experiences taught me that our lessons here must be learned in the Lord's timetable and with His guidance. Earthly learning is a process, line upon line, precept upon precept, following the example of our Savior (see D&C 98:12). With an attitude of "waiting on the Lord" (Isaiah 40:31), I learned that he truly does provide strength to face the challenge of all single-parent issues, even dating. Growing through the grief of divorce, dealing with trust questions, and sorting through a variety of relationships helped to cement a direction in my life. Without gathering information through dreary, dreaded, or even delightful dating experiences, I would have been unprepared for my successful courtship with Russell. It took that collection of dating adventures to prepare for the positive situation I now enjoy.

Retire from cautious tiptoeing along the ocean shore and embrace an attitude of swimming out with the breaking waves. I promise you that the process of stretching to increase your experiences works whether you eventually find a partner to swim with or not. You will be blessed with renewed commitment to the Lord, to your children and to yourself as you gain courage and trust to direct your life under the guidance of our Heavenly Father.

Career—Who Me?

Coping with the rash produced when you realize that you have to go to work

The starch crackled as I slipped into the cotton shirt, a stiff statement of the attention provided by a commercial laundry service. I tugged at the button on the business suit waistband. With a deep breath from me it stretched into the buttonhole. I grabbed my tailored jacket, glanced at the mirror to affirm the makeup application or the removal of a stray curler, and pronounced myself ready for an important day at the office.

After the morning mayhem I was running late, but Emily, my nine-year-old, was usually five minutes later. I fussed at her, grabbed her lunch and backpack, and headed for the garage. After the predictable delay she climbed in and buckled up, and we raced out the driveway. Only a quick stop to leave her at school, and I would be off to another day's responsibilities at work.

My first appointment was an interview with the managing partner of a Big Six accounting firm. He was a referral from the hospital's Healthy Heart rehabilitation program, an appropriate subject for a February National Heart Month food feature story. His office was in a downtown high rise, only a block from my own.

As I left the newspaper office, conscious of the time and the destination, I continued at a dashing pace: across the intersections on yellow lights and nearly sprinting to arrive with acceptable lateness. With only seconds to spare until my appointment, I stopped abruptly in my tracks as I entered the lobby of the office building. A glance to my left revealed a life-size reflection—it was me, in a business suit, carrying a briefcase and a planner. I turned to look straightforward at the mirrored lobby reflection. I did recognize the face, even the suit had a familiar appearance, but the total picture left me startled.

Who was that middle-aged woman in a business suit? Confusion engulfed my mind as I attempted to sort through the reflected image. It was me—me, the mother of six babies, car pool driver extraordinaire, laundress, housekeeper (including toilet scrubber), church and community service giver, and number one chocolate chip cookie baker. I felt like I was playing dress up; the sight I saw in the mirror utterly failed to reflect my life as I viewed it.

My response baffled me, pushing buttons of emotional response long buried in the struggle to survive. After all, it wasn't my first day on the job. I'd been working nearly 18 months when I ran head first into the mirrored sight. As it happened, it was a moment of reality recognition.

I was a working mother.

Of course, we're all working mothers, but there I was, actually working outside my home at a career in journalism. I still had three children at home and two nearby in college, though gratefully they were eating elsewhere most of the time. I'd spent 22 years as a stay-at-home working mom, the blessed type that was economically enabled to bake cookies and volunteer my time and energy on my own terms. That was before the D-word entered my financially secure existence. After years in a temple marriage, I was divorced, living in a family home I couldn't afford and faced with finding outside employment.

The Lord must have known I would need extra help in this redirection. Such an unexpected turn of events violated my eternal plans. I pleaded with the Lord to help me find work that would sustain me and my children but allow me the continued blessing of mothering (including a physical reminder of my role—the perpetual supply of freshly baked cookies). It was not the kind of intense inquiry I'd made previously, when events had become disconnected in my life. This was a totally different type of plea—I was alone and the emotional survival of my family depended on me. I felt as though the burdens were more than I could bear. I begged to understand what direction I should take. I had significant decisions to make, but felt completely inadequate after a lifetime of following the career decisions of my former spouse. Could I make such a critical decision? I needed a job that worked with my mothering goals, especially since I was alone with the children. I also required a regular income and a benefits package. It seemed like an oversized request, but I knew the Lord had promised answers to prayers (see 2 Nephi 32:5).

Blessed be my Heavenly Father for his guidance and instruction. I often recalled a phrase of scripture, "if ye are prepared ye shall not fear" (D&C 38:30). And blessed be my parents for their previous years of guidance and emphasis on education. Despite scriptural and spiritual reassurances, I was still afraid to move ahead with decisions.

Unlike many who find themselves in a midlife divorce crisis, I was prepared to return to the work force even though I hadn't worked full-time for more than 20 years. Based on continuing education years in college courses, I still had a current Utah teaching certificate. For some unknown reason, I combined those credits with other graduate hours and earned a master's degree in April before my husband left in October. I'd never intended to work full-time but thought it was timely for me to wrap up a graduate degree. Notwithstanding my lack of recent work experience, at least I was relatively current and connected in my field.

After consulting with someone in a professional career placement service and taking a battery of aptitude and interest tests, I began the search for employment. I combed news-

paper ads regularly, calling any that seemed remotely related to my training. Before making a call or sending a resume, I called the placement service for relevant information—names of contact people, history and functions of the
company, or any other inside information I could gather.
Every single response was negative; I didn't get one interview in more than 40 attempts. I reluctantly decided to go to
school districts. With my emotional stability stretched and
cracking, I lacked both confidence and endurance to face a
classroom of students every day. Over the holidays I received
two junior high school "start-within-four-days" offers. Despite the encouragement of family and friends, I turned them
both down. I couldn't face the task of teaching at that time.

   With a new year approaching and a new life ahead, I then
took a cautious plunge. Contacts through friends led me to a
position as an interior designer apprentice, a job with no
salary and no benefits, but lots of potential. In a personally
supportive environment, I began a new lifestyle as an employed mother. I cried almost every day, but there were two
other divorced women in the office to listen or supply tissues.

   As the weeks passed, my personal challenges seemed
lighter as I immersed myself in learning of my new professional responsibilities. I was still frightened, but each day
seemed easier than the previous one and my confidence
slowly expanded.

   About the time my conviction finally sprouted that I
might be successful as a designer, I received a call from the
employment specialist I had counseled with previously. He'd
made an interview appointment for me the next day, and I
was to arrive at 9:00 A.M. More tears and emotional unhing-
ing, but I followed through on his instructions.

   In the new job search, I did everything wrong: I cried uncontrolled at an initial interview (the human resources director asked me what my goals were for the next year and the
next five years—didn't he know I was lucky to get out of bed
on any given day?), and I failed to follow up on the interview

until pushed by the employment counselor. Even then, I asked only one question, "Have you made a decision about a new food editor?" When told "No," I quickly hung up. I asked only one inappropriate question at a second interview, then panicked when, surprisingly, the job offer came forward.

I met with the bishop, and he counseled me to accept the position. After all, he reasoned, it came with a generous benefits package and a salary every two weeks. Did it occur to my trusty bishop that I had never written anything for publication except a technical thesis or that I preferred not to cook? How could I write two food feature stories each week? My previous writing experience included writing weekly letters to a missionary son, occasional messages to my relatives, and the annual family summary circulated at Christmas. How could I compose ideas for a newspaper then circulated to 80,000 homes?

With an enormous step of personal courage, fortified by spiritual confirmation and a large measure of trust in the priesthood counsel, I accepted the position as a food editor of the local daily paper. My emotional anxieties increased as my confidence level fell, but I knew this was a position I could learn to do. I only wondered how I would rise to the challenge of writing each week.

My new assignment allowed flexibility beyond my wildest hopes: I researched and wrote at home in the early morning hours before the day began for the children. I wrote in the evenings when the kids were involved in their homework. Even family grocery shopping and meal preparation contributed to my workload as I tested recipes for publication. Required time in the office was limited so that much of my assignment could be done at home or at least in cooperation with the children's schedules. I still drove car pools, volunteered for classroom activities, witnessed sporting events, and baked cookies—now many more varieties than my staple chocolate chip recipe. Through the flexibility of my hours, I could generally be home when the children were home or available for the inevitable daily crisis.

The Lord's generous blessings prevailed in my individual circumstance. When faced with a perplexing situation, I often admonished the children that the Lord would help us solve the problem. I didn't know how, but I knew that someone would appear to help us uncover a solution. Time and time again, resource people assisted us as we established a new definition of family living.

I was a career woman, but my career had a dual emphasis. It was not the career I envisioned, not even the career I had academically trained for, but I found a position that provided essential services for my family. In that discovery, I also renewed my confidence to meet the challenges presented in my single-parent lifestyle.

Just as the Lord guided my professional and personal journeys, I know he will do the same for each of you. Your problems and solutions differ, your opportunities and experiences vary, but the fundamental truths of the gospel prevail when you work to apply them in any needful circumstance. Let people help you in every way possible, utilize resources you have available, and prepare yourself for a career in addition to the preparations for motherhood.

I encourage you to adhere to scriptural counsel, particularly these words of Nephi that I adopted as a personal motto: "Wherefore, ye must press forward with a steadfastness in Christ, having a perfect brightness of hope, and a love of God and of all men. Wherefore, if ye shall press forward, feasting upon the word of Christ, and endure to the end, behold, thus saith the Father: Ye shall have eternal life" (2 Nephi 31:20).

A "perfect brightness of hope" restored my energy and my faith many times as I learned the lessons of my circumstance. I understood the reality of such a promise, not only for eternity but also for the everyday challenges of this life. When single mothers face their responsibilities with that hope and with steadfastness, unexpected doors open and necessary solutions are uncovered, enabling the family to "press forward" together and succeed in every way.

Independent Steps

Soothing ointment for treatment of the emergency-room feeling of having a rebellious child

The toddler disappeared! After 15 minutes of desperate searching in the Smithsonian Air and Space Museum, our family, including my visiting-from-out-of-state parents, failed to locate two-year-old Jared. As we gathered to compare notes at the base of the Apollo rocket, we heard a cheerful voice from high above. "Hi, Grandpa," Jared shouted as he hung through the railing two stories high. "Don't move," I called, hoping that his boundless energy wouldn't propel him through the rails and onto the floor below. As I waited breathlessly, my husband raced to the back staircase to rescue the wandering boy. Jared, delighted with his apparent freedom, followed the observation line into the rocket body. Curiosity ruled as his father arrived for the rescue. Completely unaware of the turmoil regarding his disappearance, Jared began a nonstop series of questions about the rocket's operation.

As a youngster, Jared stretched his limits and discovered a sense of freedom in independent exploration. Totally oblivious to the mounting concern for his whereabouts, Jared pursued his own agenda—at two years old.

On another occasion, four-year-old Jeffrey captured his week-old baby sister and carried her by the neck down the stairs and out through the front door. When a neighbor friend beckoned, Jeff dropped Amy by the mailbox and went to locate his bicycle. Moments later, my mother, on duty while I was trying to catch up on sleep, heard Amy's cries and rescued her from the kidsnatching.

Either sibling rivalry or genuine pride may have motivated Jeff to thoughtlessly abduct his newborn sister. When another activity presented itself, Jeff moved on and Amy was abandoned in the grass.

Children often make choices that affect their own well-being as well as the safety of others. Before the age of accountability, they fail to recognize the consequences of such choices. Parents must intercede with limits that provide guidance and safety.

The age of accountability, however, redirects the responsibility for choices and consequences. A child then becomes aware of correct principles and grows in his capacity to make choices.

Accident prevention and positive reinforcement of values govern parental routines in the molding years of childhood. As the Prophet Joseph Smith counseled, "I teach them correct principles and they govern themselves."

As a mother, I've pondered when the teaching process ends and the individual governing responsibility begins. Scriptural instruction indicates that teaching the first principles of the gospel must be done as the child prepares for baptism (see D&C 68:25). Could I terminate my responsibilities if each of my children were baptized into the Church on their eighth birthday? What a miraculous solution for a mother!

Unfortunately, the responsibility to teach correct principles continues for a lifetime as the independence and knowledge of the child increases.

If I could write daily agendas for each of my five children and those agendas would be followed line by line, my life would be simplified. I would dictate a regime of diligence in righteous pursuits, prescribe a solid work ethic, and determine opportunities for service. Well, you know whose rejected plan that was—but some days it seems the only plan that brings peace of mind to a mother.

Toddler and preschool mishaps generally fall into a category labeled "controlled catastrophes." Even elementary school misadventures loom as possibilities for parental management. But watch out when junior high and adolescence arrive!

Stretching and testing become everyday exhibits in children's teenage behavior; mothers then appropriately select that developmental phase as the time for Miss Clairol to repair the increased gray hair, psychological therapy, or personal escape to Bora Bora.

In place of a tropical retreat or self-inflicted orange hair, I've learned to listen to the identity-seeking children. Listening to their words must be coupled with listening to their actions. Teenagers speak with gestures, body language, attitude, and sometimes meaningful words. With careful observations, you find you can actually communicate with an independence-seeking child. It's not easy, nor does it work consistently, but occasionally you detect a message that's meaningful.

When my 16-year-old son crashed the car into another vehicle for the second time in as many months, I notified him that his privilege to join his friends at the beach for spring break would be rescinded. He needed to work off his citations and make a contribution to the car repairs. As the time approached for the beach journey, his father was away on business and I was bedridden from a back injury. When Jeff came to talk to me about the trip, I sensed his determination to join his friends. He didn't communicate that message in words, but I had a feeling he was on his way to the coast despite my reminder of his obligations at home. A couple of hours later, a younger sister asked about the whereabouts of the car. Of course, neither the car nor the boy arrived home that evening or the next. In fact it was four days before I could locate parents who had information about the beach condo and its telephone number. Short of calling the police to report the vehicle stolen, I had little option but to wait for Jeff's return.

Jeff's escape was only one of many experiences I've had in learning how to live with the choices my children make.

Now, ten years later, I don't remember what I did when he finally returned home. Funny thing, he doesn't remember either. Maybe that's a valuable lesson in perspective.

But I do remember how I worried, how I prayed, and how I ached for a peaceful feeling regarding his whereabouts. That's the same kind of feeling I've experienced over and over again when children have implemented their agency to experiment with life. Sometimes the pain caused by their decisions creates a long-term anguish, a kind of quiet throbbing that surfaces in my personal quiet times.

There's nothing I can do in such cases but fall to my knees once again and share the burdens with the Lord. I pray that I have taught correct principles, but the test comes in the individual child's implementation of those principles. Their individuality brings varied interpretations and "wham!"—they make their own decisions! Why is it so difficult to understand why they do so when we know we agreed to the plan presented by our Savior?

Elder Richard G. Scott counseled in a conference address to "keep perspective." "When you have done all that you can reasonably do, rest the burden in the hands of the Lord." Elder Scott used a small pebble as an example. If the pebble is placed directly in front of your eye, vision is blocked and you cannot see. "When the things you realistically can do to help are done, leave the matter in the hands of the Lord and worry no more. Do not feel guilty because you cannot do more. Do not waste your energy on useless worry." If, on the other hand, you drop the pebble to the ground, it becomes smaller and you will have a clarity of vision. As time passes, the problem will find definition. "In time," Elder Scott added, "you will feel impressions and know how to give further help. You will find more peace and happiness, will not neglect others that need you, and will be able to give greater help" (*Ensign*, May 1988, p. 60).

Such inspired words of consolation and encouragement bless mothers with understanding when children choose a different path.

Linda Jacobson Eyre

Linda Eyre was born in Montpelier, Idaho to two saints—Roy and Hazel Jacobson—he a farmer, and she a school and music teacher. She was placed in the middle of an interesting and rather complicated family history. When she was born, her father was 54 and her mother 41. Roy had been married previously to a woman who had died of cancer and had two grown children. Hazel, having married for the first time at 38, decided after two years as Roy's wife that she would never be able to have biological children, so they adopted five-year-old Lloyd from an orphanage. Almost immediately, Linda popped into the picture, and the following year her younger sister and best friend, Lenna, arrived.

Linda met Richard Eyre while they were both attending Utah State University. They married and moved the same week to Boston, where Linda taught music and after two years Richard received his MBA from Harvard Business School. Since their marriage they have lived in Washington, D.C.; England (where Richard was serving as the England London South Mission President); Salt Lake City, with extended stays with their children in Mexico, learning that you don't have to have shoes to be happy; the Blue Mountains of Oregon, building a log cabin; Japan, learning that there are very different ways to think; Romania, working in an orphanage; and Wales, learning that there is still quiet somewhere.

Together they have published several books on parenting and life balance and now do writing and speaking while they continue to be full-time parents. They have nine children.

Linda loves reading, traveling, horse riding, time to be alone, and watching kids.

A Leap of Faith

Recommending a prescription of faith in dealing
with trials of missionaries, matriarchs, and moms

It seems like only yesterday that I was trying to find
boxes to store toys in just before a move. Now I find myself
packing boxes of memories. After our second ride home from
the Missionary Training Center in seven days, all of us feeling a little sorry that it wasn't as wild and crowded as our vehicle had been on the way down when we were all stuffed together with missionary and gear, we knew that this was the
end for a while. A few minutes earlier we had walked out the
front door and Saydi out the back of one of the big yellow cement rooms at the MTC built for goodbyes. "Spain will never
be the same," we said as we smiled through our tears and
watched her go. The week before it had been our strapping
6'5" Jonah, on his way to London, with his wide-open smile
and perpetual enthusiasm whom we saw walk through that
door through the tears.

I looked at Saydi's room with a sigh, knowing that if I didn't
pack up all her things that evening it would only get harder.
Melancholy was the best word I could think of to describe my
mood as I packed up Saydi's "stuff." Sweet sorrow abounded
and years flashed before my eyes as I looked through Saydi's
beautifully crafted high school and Wellesley scrapbooks: she
always seemed to be directly in the center of each picture
with that beaming smile. (Isn't it funny that our own child
somehow seems to be the star of every group picture?) Next I

moved on to Jonah's room and again marveled at the differences between kids raised in the same house with the same parents. He had already carefully packed and labeled all his boxes before he left to prepare them for their two years of storage. I lovingly picked up Jonah's Jerusalem scrapbook from his study abroad experience in the land of the Savior, which he had completed just a few weeks before. I took a few minutes to complete that little segment of his life by adding the pictures we had just had developed of the last family reunion, only two weeks earlier. Then came the exciting double farewell and the bravely smiling photos taken at the tearful last farewell at the MTC the week before.

We have attended so many farewells lately that I can't help thinking of my favorite painting at the Tate Gallery in London called "The Last Farewell." I have stood in front of it twice now, reduced both times to a puddle of tears as I see something a little more touching, a little more gripping each time. In this beautiful painting, an immigrant family with one small wagon—a mother and father and six small children—are poised on the brim of a verdant hill somewhere in Europe and are turning to wave goodbye to everything they had known: family, friends, their fields and animals, homes, and grandparents. I can still see dozens of well-wishers on the distant hills with arms raised to say goodbye to the little family whom they will probably never see again. I am especially moved by this picture because it reminds me so much of my great-great-grandparents: after joining the Church in Denmark, they and their children left everything they had known. Their oldest daughter had just passed away and had been buried on one of those green hills. Of the five remaining children they began their journey with, three died in a measles epidemic on the boat and were buried at sea. A fourth died just as they sighted land; she was buried on American soil. These wonderful, faithful parents arrived in the "promised land" with only one of the six beautiful children they had been blessed with. What a leap of faith these wonderful early Saints took, and what a price they had to pay for the cause of Zion!

Our sacrifice at the MTC seemed so small as that painting with those arms raised for the last time on that brilliant green hillside flashed in my mind when Jonah and Saydi similarly raised their arms for their last farewell. Our children were experiencing their own leap of faith as they set off for their promised lands. How much easier it was for us to let them go, knowing that they would be back in 18 months or two years. Nonetheless, these farewells possess their own kind of hard: we know by now (on our numbers 4 and 5 missionaries) that they are really saying goodbye to their childhoods and somewhat to their dependence on parents and other people's opinions. They are off in part to find out who they really are.

Having never experienced a full-time mission myself, I was glad for my own "leap of faith" experienced just the week before. Richard's brother and his wife (Chris and Hedy) and children arrived from a cross-country trip and were jubilantly looking forward to their annual favorite activity in Salt Lake City—bungee jumping. We have a spectacular 80-foot tower only 15 minutes from our home. This was certainly not *my* idea of a good time, but our kids love it and their kids love it. On the drive out, Chris and Hedy decided that it was their year to try it. You can guess what happened next—they started begging me, the chicken of the world, to try it. After planting a firm "no" on everybody several times and explaining that I've always had a terrible fear of heights and my jumping would be absolutely impossible, I started thinking. I hadn't taken a real risk for a long time. My life was filled with endless responsibilities, experiences, and challenges, but all the outcomes seemed pretty predictable. Maybe I needed to know how it felt to take a real leap of faith.

With cousins and our children wildly cheering, I finally began filling out the liability release form and could not believe that I was paying $21 to scare myself to death. I was so glad they had posted a sign above the cash register that said, "Bungee jumping may cause injury or death!" which I noticed as I put my credit card back in my purse—perhaps for the last time.

I climbed the stairs in disbelief. When I got to the top, I became preoccupied with our 10-year-old, who had jumped off the previous year with ease (after being pushed). This year pushing was off limits, and she had stood on the edge for an eternity with a long line behind her; she was unable to jump. The woman in front of me had decided to go over the edge head first with the cord tied to her feet. Somehow that was not very comforting to me. Besides it took more time. Thinking time.

At last it was my turn, and I really couldn't see losing face and faith by backing out at that point. But I also couldn't believe that I could actually do it. Chris and Hedy were telling me not to look down and *not* to stop once I got to the edge. I imagined how it would feel to put all my faith in one long stretchy cord and freely fall off this 80-foot tower. I was glad that Chris had told me that it wasn't a good time to lie about my weight. My life depended on what my weight would do to that one single cord. The technician started counting down . . . 5, 4, 3, 2 . . . and I believed I knew what it would be like to walk the gangplank to a watery grave to provide dinner for the alligators. The rush of fear and simultaneous exhilaration of doing something really risky, yet tied to a bond of faith at the very same moment, was indescribable. In the few seconds from the edge of the jump to the bottom of the first spring back up, I knew how it felt to be born, to jump off that heavenly realm and come into a scary, exciting new world, how it must have felt to our ancestors to turn around and walk away from everything they'd known on that hill in Europe. I also knew how it must feel to walk out that back room at the MTC, having forsaken family, friends, telephone calls, four-wheeling trips, and many other freedoms because of the determination to go over the edge for the Lord.

As I hit bottom and realized that I had done it and come out alive, I couldn't remember when I'd had so much fun in a few short seconds. When the big metal carabineer that was looped over my right shoulder came up and popped my front tooth on the second bounce, I thought of motherhood. Giving birth also is like going over the edge. (It is also the only other time I can think of when you have to tell somebody exactly how much you weigh.) We know that there are risks, but the rewards far outweigh the bumps. Realizing that it was even more scary for those matriarchs of old, I thought of the leap of faith it would take to give birth without anesthesia, often with nothing but an old blanket in the back of a covered wagon. Though the dangers were more physical for them, the danger still abides today. When we all congregate in heaven, I am sure that we'll all agree that motherhood is some ride!

On the way home, as I looked back from the ground at that 80-foot tower, now wearing a fat lip but still an intact tooth, I thought I had actually learned quite a bit for my $21. I had learned that life is just one leap of faith after another, but some leaps are bigger and farther than others. I also think I now know a little better how it will feel to raise my arm in a final farewell when I leave this frail existence and leap into eternity, knowing that I've fought a good fight, that I've learned some things well. I also relearned that my greatest blessings on earth will come from having experienced this life with my eternal family—both those magnificent souls who came from those green hills far away and those valiant spirits who are going back to those same hills to challenge others to take that same grand "leap of faith."

On Gazing into Each Other's Eyes

Enlightening for those who need a decongestant for their marriage

My husband and I have just celebrated our 27th wedding anniversary. I look back on those incredible years with Richard with nostalgia, wonder, and even mirth, beginning with our wedding day on July 30, 1969. We had decided that *pizazz* was one of "our words," so we wanted to do everything a little different. I have to giggle a little when I remember that this included having legal-envelope-size wedding invitations hand printed by one of our best friends whom we thought of as an artist. Each envelope was hand sealed with purple sealing wax.

My dress had an empire waist, which made me look like someone straight out of *Princess Bride* who was already pregnant. (This befuddles me as I actually was pregnant seven out of the next sixteen years. You'd think I could wait.) My colors, of course, were purple and blue, which meant the bridesmaids wore blue satin dresses with purple chiffon flowing from their own empire waists. Come to think of it, we all looked pregnant. The cake—which they told me *had* to be a fruit cake (which I hated) because there were four days between the reception and open house and anything else would surely be spoiled—sat on a purple velvet cloth with little white Christmas tree lights around it.

Most important, at the "sign-up desk" was a picture of Richard and me gazing off into the woods, under which we had posted this profound statement: *Love does not consist of gazing into each other's eyes, but of looking forward together in the same direction.*

Twenty-seven years down that path from which we could both see the goal—which, defined in its broadest terms, was to broaden and contribute and return to our Heavenly Father through experiencing the divine roles of partner and parent—I have learned even more than I bargained for! First and foremost I have learned that every marriage is different. Since no two people are the same, of course, each marriage is as different as the sum of its parts.

I mentioned at the first that I look back at our marriage with wonder. This is because (1) without *really* knowing Richard, I married someone who was absolutely perfect for me. Only years can teach you the intimate intricacies of living with someone, and through our years together I have learned and changed and grown beyond my wildest dreams. (2) It is a miracle that two such strong-willed people could tolerate each other this long! (Twenty-seven down—eternity to go!)

One of the main things that I now know is that perfect does not mean easy. Yes, we were looking forward together in the same direction. We did have goals that we set together from the very start—intricate, detailed, bold goals, which we went so far as to put on a mobile that Richard invented and hung above our bed, like over a baby's crib only bigger. When that crumbled, we made them into charts and then slides that we watched together every Sunday night. The long-range goals were the same, but we each had our own ways of reaching those goals. Because since we first met we had spent most of the time arguing, we weren't too surprised that differences of opinion did not stop the day we got married. It seems that we each were always certain that our way to accomplish the same goal was most assuredly the only true way.

Luckily we don't disagree on any of the "big stuff" such as the importance of the gospel in our lives and the commitments that it brings. Also I am so blessed to be married to an undying romantic. There is always a poem on my birthday, on our anniversary, and after most really big arguments, and there are exciting dates to far-away places, so you must understand that I'm not complaining, just explaining that there are also drawbacks to being married to such a rightbrained person. He doesn't do details. My dear Richard is a visionary man who can easily see the big picture. Answers to complicated questions are so simple to him. In addition, he is wise and has impeccably amazing judgment on the big things—which gives him the false notion that he is right about all things.

The following is just one example. Richard likes to turn old clichés around to update and improve them to accommodate life as it really is. Most concepts I fully embrace and advocate, like, "Don't just do something, sit there" and "If a thing's just barely worth doing, just barely do it!" But there is one turned-around cliché in his pocket of philosophies that is about to drive me crazy: "Play before work." Now, don't misunderstand. People usually bring philosophies of their lives from their own family experience. Richard came from an extremely hard-working widowed mother, and siblings who all know the value of work, as does Richard. It's just that the order of work and play came by his own desires and design. Having come myself from a hardworking farm family, this is very hard for me to accept. He has to have a game of tennis before he can really settle down to work, and he thinks a good movie will relax him enough to start thinking.

With the firm belief that we are here first and foremost to enjoy life, Richard has no patience with pulling out weeds, picking up toys, doing dishes, mopping floors, or cooking. I, on the other hand, believe that life is hard and complicated and that it's doubtful that there will be much time for unadulterated fun. I call the complications of raising kids fun. He calls water skiing and playing tennis fun. He finds time for both but not the details. I like working myself to death and always trying to do *everything* that needs to be done.

Of course, this is a two-way irritation. When I tell him that I really can't go to a movie because we're feeding ten thousand the next day, he can't figure why I can't get someone else to do the dirty work so I can go with him. He calls me "Martha" and thinks I am careful and troubled about many things—always feeding people, cleaning things, pulling out weeds.

I truly envy Richard's ability to literally *not* see what needs to be done. When I walk in the door, I see the crumbs on the floor, dirty dishes in the sink, and the bathroom sinks and mirrors spattered with toothpaste. He sees the food in the fridge and the *Newsweek* on the back of the toilet. While I was in the midst of writing this article, nineteen teenagers showed up unexpectedly for breakfast (circumstances too complicated to explain). As I was sweating over a pancake grill that suddenly wouldn't get hot (now that I needed to make about eighty pancakes in a hurry!) and trying in the meantime to heat two large frying pans to supplement the supply, and burning batter to a crisp because it seemed like hotter would be faster, Richard came into the kitchen with his plate full of pancakes. "Ah! He's seen my predicament and has come to the rescue," I rejoiced, just as he said, "Now, dear, where did you put that raspberry syrup?" If daggers could kill . . . he knew right away that something was wrong!

On the other hand, I can see too many things that need to be done. Richard's right when he says I've gone *too* far on fixing and cleaning and clearing. I realized that one day when I found myself mopping the floor in the rest room in an airplane. I hate it when I see the smudges on the sliding glass doors instead of the beautiful trees and flowers just beyond and when I can't enjoy unexpected company when the kitchen where we are standing looks like somebody has just thrown in a hand grenade. But I'm working on it. And when Richard sees me really trying to change, he works at changing too.

Last night, after getting to the end of a long list of "have to dos," I announced that someone else was going to have to do dinner. (We were far away from any hope for fast food.) At about 10:15 P.M. Richard passed me in the hall and with a puzzled look on his face said, "Am I mistaken or did we not have dinner tonight?" With a wide grin and arms outstretched I said, "Meet the new Mary!" In turn, he is training the kids to ask what they can do to help and agrees that it is important for them to learn to see what needs to be done.

Before that fateful wedding day, I knew that there were things about Richard that I would just have to change. I smile at myself now as I realize once again that life is hard. In order to change things in a household or a marriage, *you* are the one who has to change. Even as I learn to walk past messes and go to a movie when I'd rather stay home and clean, Richard does make the bed (sort of) and seldom leaves his own things out. We try to help each other to change, without a lot of luck. He suggests that when there is a great deal of work to do, I find someone else to do it—like he does. (He gets this bad habit from having a wonderful secretary and kids that don't dare say no.) I suggest that he try to see what needs to be done and do it *himself.* He thinks that is foolish, but he's starting to try it once in a while anyway, just to please me.

I should remember to count my blessings. In the summer, we live by a neighbor who waxes his tractor and goes crazy when one of our tennis balls messes up the level of the turf on his lawn. Things could be worse. I could be married to him! Horrors! The other day we had a high school Board of Control party at our home. The new student body and class officers had just finished a meal and were cleaning up. The student body president was diligently helping to clean up. He kept asking questions about where this went and how to put that away. Finally he said, "There I go again. I'm just like my dad—always doing *more* than really needs to be done." It made me realize that everyone has their problems!

The biggest problem in dealing with the little things that bother us about our mates is that they are like bramble bushes directly on the path to our goal. Satan often sees the opportunity to slip in and make it hard to keep our eyes on the long-range goal. He would love to confuse us and use anger and resentment to force us to think we have to take separate paths for a while or to make it harder because of the underbrush to see the goal as clearly as we should.

What I find myself doing is being so angry sometimes at the little things that I forget to remember the big things—the things I love most about Richard—and to remind him of them too. My favorite word from the scriptures this year is *remember*. That word shows up over and over again in admonitions from remembering the sacrifice of the Savior to remembering the sabbath day to keep it holy to remembering our ancestors. The word *remember* appears 360 times in the standard works. One of the most important things we must remember is a commitment to a good marriage . . . whatever it takes.

In our partnership one of our greatest assets (although it sometimes seems like a trial) is Richard's insistence that we communicate our bad feelings consistently and thoroughly. If we don't have time to talk about bad feelings on the spot, we let each other know our feelings later and have been known to stay up into the wee hours of the morning working to an acceptable solution for us both. Then on fast Sunday we always try to have a private testimony meeting wherein we begin by saying something we admire or appreciate about the other before we let the other know the things that have really bothered us since we last talked. Sometimes when we just can't get good feelings about our relationship we go to the last place we feel like going—to our knees. We find ourselves beginning by saying, in essence, "Please help this stupid bullheaded person realize how wrong he is," and then through the blessed, reliable Spirit of the Lord, we end up saying in essence, "Please forgive us for not seeing the other person's point of view sooner." It is a great lesson in the power of negotiation by the Spirit.

No one could possibly have predicted all the wild and wonderful, trying and terrible things that would happen to

Richard and me by the time we had turned the 6 and 9 of that July day in 1969 around to 1996. On our first anniversary our firstborn, Saren, came into the world; eight more incredible, wonderful, challenging spirits followed to make our lives brim with joy as we struggled with juggling life and all the accompanying broken bones, broken windows, and broken hearts. We used the purple velvet tablecloth from our wedding for a funeral shroud for our beloved little cocker spaniel. Last anniversary my 89-year-old mother had a heart attack and died 48 hours later. This anniversary was one day before we delivered our fifth missionary to the MTC. Yet Richard still found time to take me off for a little four-wheeling adventure to the nearby mountains, where we enjoyed a simple picnic in a pretty basket filled with cheese and crackers and fruit and sparkling juice and mineral water . . . and a poem. A romantic forever.

I love this man eons more than I thought possible 27 years ago, despite his weaknesses (and my strengths). Everyone has his or her pet irritations about their spouse, which makes marriage hard. But hard is good—the best—especially when you realize that you not only have to look forward together in the same direction but also you have to proceed to the goal no matter what it takes.

One other thing. I have realized that romantic love should never get lost in the bog. Besides looking forward together, maybe just as important is the fact that love *does* consist of looking into each other's eyes . . . and *remembering* that vital, burning love.

Torn-to-Pieces-Hood

Putting the everyday tornado in perspective

Ah! What sweet bliss it would be to just go to an orderly, tastefully decorated, peacefully quiet office to write. With a cheerful secretary outside my door who could take, defer, or delay calls until I found the appropriate moment to return them and with someone else at home cleaning and cooking, I could accomplish wonders! Instead, it seems that I have been trying *forever* to find that appropriate moment in the hectic confusion of everyday pandemonium to sit down and write. Something that needs to be done or someone who needs my attention always seem to be figuratively, and sometimes literally, screaming in my face.

I love the phrase that Anne Morrow Lindbergh uses in her great classic, *Gift from the Sea*. She describes motherhood with a new term: *Zerreissenheit,* a German word which translated literally means "torn-to-pieces-hood." When you contemplate the content of the typical day of a mother, is this not often the overriding emotion?

The last time I had time to write, I was confined to an airplane, which I love. No one calls on the phone, someone else brings *you* food, and you really shouldn't have to worry about cleaning the bathroom. On the plane I visualized returning to our battered kitchen and decided it was time to revitalize it a bit, considering it has endured fifteen years of brutal beating. What seemed at the moment on that peaceful airplane ride like a simple task turned into a nightmare as I struggled to decide on a suitable countertop material and to choose the best possible stove and sink for our kitchen for the next twenty years. Next the workmen cut the hole in the countertop too large for the stove top and put the wrong finish on the floor, which means that the floor feels like sandpaper underfoot and the chairs scream every time we move them.

In the meantime, I was trying to fulfill my new ward calling as the Young Women's president with vigor and get a handle on the myriad activities that calling includes. One particular afternoon stands out as I was struggling to find something for one child to eat because he had to leave for a school activity at the same time as I was trying to find something to feed the other children for dinner, as I knew I would be gone. Meanwhile, I frantically chopped fruit into a bowl for a fruit salad on my right as I chucked lettuce into another bowl on my left for my first Young Women's activity. I had spent the whole day on the phone trying to figure out how to make everybody happy by changing location, duration, and content of the activity because of unforeseen changes in the situation—and trying to persuade girls reluctant to attend that it would be an exciting and worthwhile activity.

The appointed meeting time was 5:30, and it was now 5:15 and counting. I was literally sweating, keeping both hands flying as fast as my mind, knowing that I absolutely had to be on time for at least this first activity, when the phone rang. I ran to the phone which was supposed to be used only for family emergencies thinking, "If this is anything less than a national emergency, I am going to hang up!" My mental state was not good. On the other end of the line I heard the sweet voice of our married daughter who had recently moved to Washington D.C. Noticing just a hint of irritation in my voice, she proceeded anyway with a certain anxiousness in her voice. "Now, I know this is a little early, Mom," she said on that day in mid-May, "But I *have* to know what we're doing for Thanksgiving." After a moment of silent disbelief, I began to laugh hysterically—a cackling, uncontrolled laugh such as you'd hear in an insane asylum. "Mother!

Mother! What's wrong? What are you laughing about?" Shawni pleaded. Right then I realized that if *zerreissenheit* was torn-to-pieces-hood, I was a shred!

In mid-June our ten-year-old, Charity, and I attended a Suzuki flute camp for a week in Provo. While she was attending classes that we both were supposed to be enjoying, I found myself slipping away to call and see if the tile man had made it to the kitchen yet; to deliver things to our older daughter Saydi at BYU, where she was working as a counselor for the Especially for Youth program; and to quickly shop for those elusive white missionary shirts with size 37 sleeves. I slipped back into the flute repertoire class just before it ended.

As the summer progressed, I found myself saying, "After this event or that deadline, I'll have time to write." Yet I kept finding myself torn to pieces just trying to keep up with the everyday demands of the kids and the house. The campouts, the trips, the preparations for getting two missionaries ready for full-time service, and the Young Women activities kept me going from one crisis to another.

Finally on the other side of a family reunion, which represented the last time we'll all twelve be together for two years (having six months earlier had the last Christmas together until the year 2004 because of missionary service) and having packed in enough food to our little lake cabin for 10 meals for us 12 without having to travel an hour to the nearest grocery store and back, and then preparing a double farewell and open house for 200 afterward, and having delivered two fresh new ambassadors to the Lord and then having sent all the things they left or didn't know they'd need, we now come down to today. I'm back at our little lake cabin, listening to a song played by my teenagers while they play tennis and I write. The words go like this: "Time keeps on slipping, slipping, slipping into the future. I want to fly like an eagle to the sea. Fly like an eagle, let my spirit carry me. Fly like an eagle, till I'm free. Time keeps on slipping, slipping, slipping into the future."

This morning I decided to fly like an eagle. I got on our whiz-bang bike that I've been planning to ride for years. It's my goal to ride all the way around the lake this summer, and I needed to get in shape. I could hardly wait to feel the wind whipping through my hair and to give a wake-up call to those unsuspecting muscles in my legs and arms that are used to being used exclusively to run up and down stairs, load washers and empty dryers, and push the gas and brake pedals on the car. I walked the bike up the steep hill to the road, feeling that I really should be writing. After the first mile I began to feel exhilarated by the clean, pure mountain air. At three miles, with heart pounding and muscles stretching, even burning, I had a flat tire. The walk home was nice. I realized that the time that keeps on slipping into the future is not a lot different than it has been in the past. There are always unexpected dilemmas and surprises, always that feeling of being torn to pieces, needs flying in from every side along with guilty feelings that no matter how hard you're working, there is something else you really should be doing.

But wait. Lest you think this is a doom and gloom chapter, I have a happy ending: I thought of it when I was watching our 13-year-old, Eli, playing tennis this morning. I preface this little incident by telling you that Eli is a perfectionist, with a temper to match. He *has* to win. He *has* to know that he is doing things just right. Things *have* to go well for him or he explodes. In this particular match with his brother, he had just missed a particularly crucial point. He came running to the chain link fence, put all ten fingers through the holes, clung until his knuckles were white, and with that old familiar livid look on his face screamed at me as I sat here by the table writing, *"Why is it that every time I get to an important point, a butterfly flies in front of me?"*

After I crumpled up in laughter, I realized that Eli had given me the answer to the great dilemma of coping with zerreissenheit. All those demands and worries and schedule changes and food preparations and flat tires are really like butterflies. Sometimes we view these butterflies as necessary intrusions, sometimes as things to help us concentrate harder, and sometimes even as things of beauty that flit in and out of our lives, but they all have one thing in common—they are fleeting.

When I put those "torn pieces" of the last few months into perspective, I realize that what I will really remember about this summer are not distractions of butterflies but rather feeling joy and gratitude at hearing the firm, honest testimonies of each child at the farewell; laughing about old times with the kids while we were gathered around the old couch at the cabin; sitting in a car during a thunder and lightning storm with four Mia Maids who spontaneously taught me the gospel from the Doctrine and Covenants and expressed an urgency that each felt to teach the gospel to a good friend. I'll remember a magnificent Japanese master flute teacher putting his arm around a little girl in a master class and saying, "When you get to heaven and God comes up to you and says with excitement, 'Did you get it?' You don't want to look at him blankly and say, 'Get what?'"

By tomorrow, I won't remember that at lunch today I felt like a pesky fly being flicked off an arm when I said, "No one made their beds this morning," "Put your dishes in the dishwasher, not the sink," "Who's going to do these dishes?" and "Who would like to make dinner?" No one even seemed to hear what I said, let alone respond. What I will remember that puts all the torn pieces of the day back together is when 15-year-old Noah put his arm around me amidst the mess and asked, "What are you doing out there on the back porch, Mom?" "I'm writing a book," I replied, thinking that would flutter on by too. But instead he said, "Well, whatever you're writing, I'm sure it's great."

A peaceful, quiet office doesn't sound so great after all.

The Parable of the Sadhu

Applying an antidote for the poison of guilt

In September of 1996 Richard and I were asked to be the concluding speakers at a two-day conference on ethics and values for a gigantic corporation well-known for its years of service in providing great family entertainment. The CEO of this prestigious company and his 80 top executives were all gathered in Aspen, Colorado, for their annual conference. On the first day we were shown a 15-minute clip of a film made about a man named Buzz who had grown weary of the rat race he faced each day on Wall Street in New York and decided to take a year off to travel and put some adventure back into his life. Considering it the greatest adventure he could imagine, he decided to climb Mount Everest. For months he prepared mentally and physically for the great climb. After thousands of hours of preparation and apprehensions and then trials and tribulations along the path, we saw the climber within a short distance of his goal but in the midst of a blizzard with only a few hours left to cross an especially crucial pass before another crippling storm would hit, making it impossible to reach their goal.

Just when they thought they couldn't tolerate another complication, a very poignant one was thrust upon them. Several Australian climbers came down the path half carrying, half dragging an unconscious man whom they referred to as "the Sadhu." He appeared to be a native of the region, perhaps some sort of holy man, dressed only in a flimsy robe, whom they had found half frozen along the trail. No one knew who he was nor could they understand his language as he fluttered in and out of consciousness. Nor could anyone understand why he was there on that mountain in such terrible conditions. The Australians declared that they had done their part and that someone from Buzz's group should take him down to the base camp to save his life, and they were gone.

After conferring for a short time in the oncoming blizzard's blistering wind, two men in Buzz's group decided to take the delirious man down the slope until they found someone else who could help him, then hurry back up before they missed their last chance to cross the pass before the storm descended with all its fury. When Buzz's tent mate, who had been one of the two who had carried the Sadhu down, came panting into Buzz's tent after finding someone else to take care of the Sadhu about an hour down the trail, he was so flustered and angry at himself and the others in the group who didn't offer to help that the only thing he could say was, "How does it feel to have taken part in a man's death?" Buzz rationalized that the next group probably got him to safety.

Within minutes the climbers in Buzz's expedition were on their way to the top. Somehow they accomplished their goal, but the words of Buzz's climbing companion had burned into his heart. As he reached the summit, he suddenly realized that he had been climbing the wrong mountain. He had never really left the "win at all costs" mentality of Wall Street. Logically, he knew that a person's life was more important than any other goal, but the urgency of the moment—thoughts of time and money and training and maximum effort expended to reach his goal, to reach the top—had blurred his reasoning ability. He tried to rationalize, but he knew he had made a *big* mistake.

By the time he had reached the bottom of the mountain and for many years thereafter he knew that he committed a terrible sin of omission that would be very difficult to live with. He spent months trying to find out what had happened to the man whose life he could perhaps have saved if the monument of "achievement" hadn't been so largely blocking his view. The only information that he could glean in his search was that the next group called upon to help had passed him on to someone else. The bottom line was that "the Sadhu" was probably buried in a frozen grave somewhere on the mountain.

When the film clip concluded, a lively and intriguing discussion ensued. People exposed their own values as they discussed what had happened. To most of us, sitting in a plush, warm hotel conference room in Aspen, the error of what Buzz had done seemed so obvious. There was discussion about prejudice and the fact that the outcome would probably have been different if the person in need had been a western woman or a wealthy businessman. One participant admitted that given the circumstances we had just witnessed, he might have done the same thing. But it was easy for most of us to say that we would have done the right thing, even that we thought Buzz should have realized that the real adventure would have been taking the Sadhu back down the mountain themselves and to have experienced the thrill of finding friends or relatives who could have explained the background on this man's very interesting situation.

The most heart-wrenching part for me was talking to someone afterward who had actually known Buzz, knew that he was now a Presbyterian minister, and knew that he spent the rest of his life with a huge burden of guilt and trying to make up for his mistake with thousands of hours of love and caring to many others. I was moved by the story but had no idea that I would be confronted with my own little Sadhu incident on the following day in a little different way.

Richard and I had been told that this enormously prestigious company had specifically requested to have this conference on values and ethics because they felt that the lifestyles of some of the executives and sometimes the direction of the company were not in sync with its wholesome, family-oriented image. We felt an enormous responsibility to teach these executives, many of whom were wonderful people with good hearts and worthy goals, how important their job was to maintain high values in their homes as well as at the office and to portray those same values to the world. We felt, in some ways, this company was the last great hope of America (next to the Church of course). We wanted them to know that they had a great responsibility to continue to provide inspiring and uplifting material for the families of the world. Yet we were worried about some of the comments we were hearing that led us to believe that was not the intention—that the top of the mountain, no matter what, was money, that the almighty dollar was more important than anything else. That evening we were shown their newest movie, which was released under another company's name but owned and financed by them. It had some reference to ethics and twisted values, but it was extremely violent. We also knew that they had just acquired another company that was well-known for producing movies with objectionable content.

We stayed up far into the night thinking and praying about what to do and what to say. We decided to plead with these top executives on behalf of America's parents to continue to produce things that would influence families for good; to remind them that with their new acquisition of one of the three major daytime television networks, they touched the lives of millions of Americans every day; and that they probably had more influence in our homes and families than the president or congress.

On an early morning run on the day that we were to deliver our talks, Richard wrote a letter to them in an open poetry form that he felt would aptly state the plight and plea of parents everywhere. We kept praying and knew a little about how Samuel the Lamanite must have felt as he approached the city wall. The two morning presentations had been spectacular and had dealt with "Windows of Belief" and "Dealing with Conflict through Aikido," a fascinating form of Japanese martial art. After lunch, our "hour and a half" to connect with these executives and their wives and "significant others"

arrived. Our lovely Jewish friend from the inside organization who had hired us to speak, having no idea what we were
about to say, was sitting by me, telling me that she was 120
percent sure that they would love whatever it was we had to
say about family values and lifebalance.

As soon as Richard started talking about values as it applied to their company and I started to talk about truth and
light, the room started to feel dark. I guess everyone had
their own opinion of what transpired. Many looked interested
and even excited, but some were obviously not happy. The
harder I tried to feel "in sync," the darker the feeling became.
I tried to lighten things a bit with a few funny stories, but in
the end we stood as two parents pleading for the welfare of
all our children and America's children and families as
Richard concluded with his letter. Some got it and appreciated it. Many did not. Luckily, we had to leave for another
speech right away, but we knew that all were not thrilled
with what we had to say.

The mother in me took over. I went on a five-day guilt trip.
I don't know how many women do this, but I must admit that
while there are a lot of things I don't do well, I am magnificent
at guilt trips. I used to torture myself for hours after a talk in
sacrament meeting for forgetting to say something or worrying that what I had said was not clear. However, the more I
began speaking, the less time I had to worry about it. Frequently we were speaking so often that I simply had to rely on
the Spirit for guidance, and I found a way to make myself forget things that I wished I'd said or done, thinking that I could
do better next time. If people listening had the Spirit, I reasoned, they would "feel" what I was saying, and if they didn't,
it wouldn't matter what I said anyway. I reserved the major
guilt trips for the *big* things—like my mother's funeral.

She had always told us that she wanted her funeral to be
short and funny. She passed away quickly and unexpectedly.
My sister and I decided that we would participate in the program for this wonderful woman's final farewell. When it
came right down to it, I didn't feel like being funny on that

day, and there was just no way to get almost ninety years of service and love and fun into the allotted time. It was hot and I spoke too long and I could imagine her tapping her foot in heaven, saying, "Quit, Linda, quit! Enough is enough!" It took me weeks to quit worrying about how I had kept all those people too long, fanning themselves with their funeral programs in the heat. I somehow knew that Mom would forgive me, but for weeks I found it hard to forgive myself. I just love trips, and I guess that I must like the ones to the land of guilt most because I go there so often.

Now that you have the picture, you must begin to realize my reaction when I realized that I had muffed this once-in-a-lifetime opportunity to change the world with my speech to the big entertainment corporation. I couldn't eat or sleep very well for several days, wondering what I could have done to make things better. Although logically I knew that what we had done was right, I also knew that the people who had hired us and whose heads were on the line were disappointed that we had taken on the task of "crying repentance." I kept wondering if it would have changed things if I had prepared more, felt the Spirit a little differently, worn something different, told different stories, or just been funnier. I began to feel that I knew a little better how Buzz had felt about the Sadhu. I woke up with a weird feeling of depression every morning, wondering what was wrong and then remembering. I began to look for ways to divert my mind to get myself out of this self-depreciating mode.

During the sacrament service the next week, I finally decided to "cast my burden," something I so often advise my children to do but which I had not previously thought of as a way to rescue myself. During those minutes of deep and quiet contemplation, the Lord taught me that the best thing about guilt is that it motivates us to change. It is a very poignant way to help us realize that we can learn valuable lessons from what we consider our mistakes and what the Lord often deems a teaching moment. It helps us determine ways to improve and gives us a way to see the things that we can change and forgive ourselves for the things we cannot. As one mother who lost a child to drugs for several years once told me, "In retrospect, I did the best I could with the information that I had at the time." I remembered that Hugh Nibley once said that we came here to earth to learn only two things: How to repent and how to forgive. For me, however, repenting and forgiving others is so much easier than forgiving myself.

I had been so hard on myself! I smile now when I remember shuddering as I contemplated what those people in that room must have thought of me. Again in my ears rang my advice to my children when they become overly concerned about what people might think of them. The truth is that most people aren't thinking about them at all. They are too busy thinking about themselves. Ninety-five percent of the people at that seminar probably never gave our presentation another thought, though I had thought of almost nothing else for days. Those who did probably needed to give it a second thought because our bottom line message was clear—and true. It occurred to me that maybe Buzz shouldn't have worried so much either. Maybe the Sadhu went to the mountain to die. Just a thought.

Because of our propensities for love and compassion for others, women often feel guilt even when they shouldn't. This was certainly partly true of my experience with the good people at this conference. Recently, after I had finished speaking to a group of Relief Society sisters about guilt, a beautiful eighty-year-old sister, frail, but full of light, came up to me and shared a recent experience. She was in her car, stopped at a red light at a busy intersection, when a wild-eyed, tattered woman came running up to her car, frantically knocked on the window, and yelled, "You've got to let me in. I need a ride!" Something told her to push down the safety lock on all doors instead of letting the woman in. But she felt terrible as the light turned green and she drove away. "I haven't been able to sleep for weeks since it happened," she said. "What if something terrible happened to her?" You could tell that she was still in pain from feeling guilty about putting her own safety first, even though logically speaking she had certainly done the right thing.

As mothers, we are reminded so often to feel guilt over something. (If we forget, our children remind us.) So often if a child is having a problem, we find a way to make it our fault. We take the blame for their shyness, their tendencies toward procrastination, their inability to play the piano, and even their bad teeth. While there are things that we probably need to repent of and change about ourselves, which we should try to do often, we also have to remember that there are things that we cannot and should not change. Our children are not lumps of clay that we can mold into whatever shape we like. They are seedlings. We can't change an oak tree into an elm or a lemon tree into an orange tree. Children are who they are, and all we can do is be gardeners. We can try to provide good soil, fertilizer, water (but not too much), and most of all sunshine—remembering that clouds and rain are good too. We can't blame ourselves for every branch that shoots off in the wrong direction, because there is sap inside every tree that contains something called agency.

And when we do make mistakes, the thing that the Lord really wants us to do is not to beat ourselves up over them. That is Satan's plan. He was probably rubbing his hands with glee the week I spent hating myself. We must remember that clever fellow was once one of the brightest spirits in heaven. He knows exactly where to go for the "jugular" and recognizes that if he can get us down by using guilt and thoughts of low self-esteem we are in his power.

Truly one of life's challenges is to learn to repent *and* to forgive ourselves for mistakes in our past as well as the mistakes last week. What a wise and wonderful Father and Brother we have who can shoulder our burdens and give us peace! Whenever I study the scriptures, I find something that I've never really noticed before that perfectly applies to the dilemma I am having at the moment. We have once again renewed our efforts to read the Book of Mormon together as a family. We've had to be creative about times and places, but since we have two missionaries in the field at present who write every week and ask about what we are reading in the Book of Mormon, it is an absolute must. As we read in Alma about the wicked Zeezrom who had plagued Alma and Amulek for so long and then suddenly realized the error of his ways, I saw myself in him as he described the misery of guilt. Even though most of our guilt is not of quite the same degree, I felt a special closeness to his feelings because of my recent experience:

> And Zeezrom lay sick . . . with a burning fever, which was caused by the great tribulations of his mind on account of his wickedness, for he supposed that Alma and Amulek were no more; and he supposed that they had been slain because of his iniquity. And this great sin, and his many other sins, did harrow up his mind until it did become exceedingly sore, having no deliverance; therefore he began to be scorched with a burning heat (Alma 15:3).

I thought being harrowed was a very good description for what I had just been through. Then beginning in verse 5, we see the wonderful resolution of this problem when Zeezrom discovers that Alma and Amulek are alive and sends for them:

> And it came to pass that they went immediately, obeying the message which he had sent unto them; and they went . . . unto Zeezrom; and they found him upon his bed, sick, being very low with a burning fever; and his mind also was exceedingly sore because of his iniquities; and when he saw them he stretched forth his hand, and besought them that they would heal him.
>
> And it came to pass that Alma said unto him, taking him by the hand: Believest thou in the power of Christ unto salvation?
>
> And he answered and said: Yea, I believe all the words that thou hast taught.
>
> And Alma said: If thou believest in the redemption of Christ thou canst be healed.

And he said: Yea, I believe according to thy words. And then Alma cried unto the Lord, saying: O Lord our God, have mercy on this man, and heal him according to his faith which is in Christ.

And when Alma had said these words Zeezrom leaped upon his feet, and began to walk; and this was done to the great astonishment of all the people. . . .

And Alma baptized Zeezrom unto the Lord; and he began from that time forth to preach unto the people (Alma 15:5–12).

What a joy it is when we, like Zeezrom, find the error in our ways, change them if necessary, and most important stop the harrowing in our own minds and forgive ourselves for the things we may have done knowingly or inadvertently. The greatest peace on earth comes from our ability to "cast our burdens," whatever they may be, and truly be healed according to *our* faith in Christ, the Prince of Peace, as we deal with the Sadhus of our own lives.

Sibling Rivalry Revisited

Lubricating those itchy, irritating arguments that can get under your skin

I must admit that I had my doubts, but I was desperate. It seemed that most of my day was spent refereeing arguments. It was a Catch-22 situation. If I called one kid for a foul, he was furious and felt misunderstood, wronged, and deflated. Often he was so irate that I had to call a technical and send him out of the game. Meanwhile the other child was gloating about having been the one who, in his mother's eyes, was right. The more I tried to be a better referee, the worse things got. I got so tired of being the judge and jury and always coming out feeling that one child felt favored and smugly righteous while the other felt destroyed and depreciated.

After the first several years of parenting, we realized that when it came to sibling rivalry we felt that we were on some sort of weird merry-go-round, and Richard and I were ready to get off! All the fights and arguments going on constantly and all the time it took to discipline the wrongdoers was creating a spirit of contention, not only between the children but also between us as we disagreed on the degree and severity of punishment. Even though it was not always outwardly obvious, an underlying current of resentment broiled between some sets of children who particularly annoyed each other. The continual conflicts were beginning to make certain children feel that they actually didn't like a sibling very well. We thought. We prayed. We wrestled with what to do.

The worst part of it is that arguments always seemed to erupt just as things were at their worst. I'll never forget one trip from our home in Salt Lake City to our cabin at Bear Lake—supposedly a three-hour ride. We were all crammed in our old yellow-and-white suburban that the children had affectionately named "Bumblebee." We had planned to spend several weeks at the cabin for our summer getaway, so not only did we have all the children but also our hyperactive cocker spaniel; a shy, reclusive cat who hated crowds; a mother duck and six ducklings that we had hatched from eggs for a "fun" summer project; *and* a horse trailer and two horses that we were taking along to ride on the beach. (Richard thought it sounded so romantic.) Two of the children started fighting over who got to hold the cat. Just as they were about to pull the poor thing in half and I, with figurative steam coming out my ears, was about to offer Solomon's solution and cut the cat in half, we saw real steam—more like smoke, beginning to curl out of the hood of the car. (I always thought that we really should have named the old thing "Lemon.")

To make a long story short, we ended up smuggling the ducks, who are the messiest animals on the face of the earth, into a little motel room bathtub. I think we put the dog in a suitcase and the cat under somebody's coat to complete our clandestine operation to get everybody and everything into a shelter for the night while Richard hitched a ride back to Salt Lake to get another car and Bumblebee-Lemon went to the hospital for a good long stay. Even with two rooms (which was a real treat for us in those days), the children who got on each others' nerves most seemed to find each other immediately and begin their altercations. I threatened to make the next child who started a fight be the one to go out in the morning in broad daylight and remove the "horse droppings" from the back parking lot where Richard had found the furthest away, least noticeable spot to park the horse trailer for the night.

As we all know, the passage of crisis plus time equals humor. Our family still cracks up whenever we remember Jonah's face when I told him that *he* was the one who would have to accomplish the dastardly deed, and he begged for forgiveness like a man being sent to the guillotine. I'm not sure, but I think this was the deciding event that forced us to come up with a solution for sibling rivalry that would use the principles of the gospel to teach correct principles. As you can see, we were absolutely desperate. (Not that it's a good idea to wait until you're desperate to put the gospel in action.) And I also had my doubts about whether it would work.

After some trial and error and lots of fine tuning, this is what we came up with: when two children get into an argument that involves loud noises and disrupts the peace in the house, they are immediately required to go to a place we call the repenting bench. This place for repenting was formalized at our house when we brought a small, uncomfortable, old wooden pew from a church, purchased at an old furniture house in England. (But the top step of your staircase works just as well.) Here the children are required to sit by each other until they can complete the process of repentance. There is an actual dialogue that goes with the process which may sound contrived—because it is—but it does teach some important principles.

First, we tell them that they must sit there until they have figured out what they did wrong. When they complain that it was totally the other person's fault, we simply inform them that "it takes two to tangle" and that both parties are at fault if the disagreement becomes an argument. If they absolutely cannot figure out what they did wrong, they can ask the other kid, who of course always knows. When they are ready to tell Richard or me or the babysitter what they did wrong, we must, hard as it is, be ready to listen. When they have each explained what they did (Charity's favorite all-purpose answer is, "I provoked him," which is almost always true), they then have to say to the other child, "I'm sorry. Will you forgive me? I'll try not to do it again." The other child's decision about whether to forgive sometimes takes a while if feelings have really been damaged, but it is amazing how forgiving children are when confronted with the opportunity. The final part of this little ritual is for the two former foes to give each other a hug.

True, not every resolution is totally heartfelt. Also, we used to ask the children to say, "I'll *never* do it again," but we felt that since they were often at it again within an hour, we didn't want to make liars out of them. And true, not every attempt at repentance may be completely sincere. But as the years have passed, we have seen some remarkable results from using this major principle of the gospel to teach children about one of the most important things that they came here to learn.

After a training period for all of us, I was a convert. Interestingly, this little ritual taught us things we hadn't anticipated. The thought process involved in helping a child realize that he had indeed done something wrong helped them to accept guilt and take responsibility for it by asking for forgiveness, even if it was just a little thing. The hug dissipated bad feelings that only minutes before had seemed insurmountable. I had become only a facilitator and not the judge and jury. And most important, the children were becoming friends working through difficulties instead of constant rivals subject only to unfair judgments based on how mad I was and how much I knew about what had actually transpired. They became their own judge and jury. What a relief!

To this day, the greatest trials and the greatest joys at our house come because of sibling rivalry. Our last two children make the other children's rivalries look like a picnic in the park. Theirs is truly the "mother of all rivalries." Since the day Charity was born, Eli has been figuratively and literally carrying her around by the neck because doing so made her squirm and scream—his two favorite responses from her. I think he secretly resents her for taking over his very comfortable three-year position as the ogled-over, delightful youngest child in the family with the whatever-you-want-is-fine-with-us mentality. Suddenly he was simply one of the older children, and he wanted to make her pay. That, plus the fact that he came with a propensity for the gleeful feeling of power produced by teasing someone to the point of exasperation, makes this sibling rivalry particularly poignant. She in turn has developed a blood-curdling scream and could write a book called *A Thousand Ways to Annoy Eli*.

If they were sent to the repenting bench every time they had an argument, they'd have bottoms the shape of the bench. For them, we save only the family-disrupting, peace-shattering arguments for the repenting bench. For example, the other day Charity was hysterically screaming at Eli to get out of her room because he hadn't been invited in, and Eli was resolutely claiming that he had only come in to help her and he wasn't leaving until he did. With the anger ready to explode like a can of Seven-up that has been shaken, I felt the impulse to pop open the lid, as I still often do. I resorted to the repenting bench instead. It worked much better than any intervention I could have made.

One nice thing about the dilemma of sibling rivalry is being able through time to see it in perspective. Through years of helping the children to work out their problems with each other, even though, as I mentioned earlier, there were periods with the other children when I felt that two of them really didn't like each for a while, I found almost to my amazement that this wonderful principle of the gospel called repentance actually works with kids too! Although sometimes the process of the repenting bench seemed repetitive and mechanical and perhaps not entirely sincere, in hindsight I find that we have grown siblings who, different as they are, love each other fiercely. (Although they still have their moments.)

True, rivalries are also based on little jealousies along the way. One child may feel that he was upstaged or downsized because of the gifts of another, which is often the source of the arguments and bad feelings among siblings, even if it isn't verbalized at the time. This is why constant praise from a parent for things children have done well, and especially after children have worked out a disagreement successfully, is so important. Everyone needs to be validated. Nothing is more important than telling Eli that I know he's a good person inside, even though he has just "accidentally" wandered into Charity's room to "help" her, even though he knew it would probably make her mad.

Of course, there are many reasons for sibling rivalries. Some are a result of parents' perceptions of how kids stack up against each other and the children's consequential insecure feelings to "be as good as Elizabeth" or "be the best" and "win at all costs." That is another whole chapter. I'm not proposing that the repenting bench is the answer to all sibling rivalry problems and especially not the perfect way to deal with rivalries when you may not have had a repentance process when your children were young. You may now have worries about dealing with rivalries between teenagers or even grown children, but somehow I think that the only way to fix rivalries is to talk about them. It's amazing how responsive and communicative kids are if you get the problem out on the table, dig up some old bad feelings and talk about them, and use the process of repentance to make things better.

My second favorite scene from the scriptures is King Benjamin's address. In Mosiah 4, wonderful King Benjamin presents the most magnificent message in all the scriptures directly to parents. He presents his case for children without rivalry (among other things) in the form of a challenge and a promise. In verse 11, he challenges us to

> remember, and always retain in remembrance, the greatness of God, and your own nothingness, and his goodness and long-suffering towards you, unworthy creatures, and humble yourselves even in the depths of humility, calling on the name of the Lord daily, and standing steadfastly in the faith of that which is to come.

What follows is a list of 10 marvelous blessings the Lord promises if we accept this challenge, things that any parent would die for. Verses 14 and 15 include promises like "[our children] will not transgress the laws of God and fight and quarrel one with one other and serve the devil, who is the master of sin" and that "ye will teach them to walk in the ways of truth and soberness; ye will teach them to love one another and serve one another." These are not the challenges; these are the promises if we but accept the challenge to always remember the Lord's greatness and our nothingness as we call on him daily and stand firm in the faith.

Although there were days when I knew that I was doing something terribly wrong because it seemed that all the kids were doing was fighting and quarreling, I've learned that promises take time to come to pass. One of our best "sibling rivalists" was our darling Jonah, who is serving a mission in London. About a month after he arrived in England, he wrote an individual note to each of the children still at home that fulfilled the marvelous promises of the Lord through King Benjamin. From the farthest eastern point in England at a little village on the sea, he wrote to his siblings, whom he had formerly regarded as either great pecking posts or sniveling, pesky little irritations in his day.

To 10-year-old Charity: "It's hard to write letters very often because we are always going faster than a blender! I showed some boys your picture here, and they are all saving up money for plane tickets to America to see you. I feel happy inside when I think of you too. Make sure you have no tantrum attacks for me for just one day each week. You can even call it the 'Jonah Day.' You are such a great little sister and so grown up for your age. Don't let it go to your head, K? Be happy, Love, Jonah."

To 16-year-old Noah and 17-year-old Talmadge, he writes (among other things): "You guys have got to work hard in your new responsibilities at school and in your classes. It's so important! Also, don't get stuck with one girl when you're dating. I've seen it happen too many times. There are too many fish in the sea for that stuff! Now, you gotta listen to this last part—LISTEN IN SEMINARY. You will learn so much and it will help you so much on your mission. In addition to that, read a couple of verses every day in the Book of Mormon and you will be STRONG! I love you mates, Give joy, Jonah."

To 13-year-old Eli he writes: "You need to watch out for people who need your help. Show your friends that it's fun to be strong in what they believe. Man, missionary work is so cool! You have no idea till you actually do it but it's great. Yahoo. Eli, pray always and make sure that God knows that you love him and Jesus knows that you're grateful for his sacrifice by using the atonement. Repent of small sins and it will put you in good practice. You are the man! Share happiness, Jo (your bodyslammer)."

Though I've come to believe that sibling rivalry is part of raising more than one child at the same time, I also believe that it's never over until it's over. At present, our five who have left home are each other's truest friends. I now believe that not only is rivalry a blessing while it is happening as you learn to cope with different personalities and how they fit into the framework of the gospel, but it also is one of the greatest joys as you see children emerge with a sense of fervent love for each other *because* of what they've been through in their "baptism by fire." (Excuse me—I've got to go see why Charity is screaming.)

Moms Just Need to Have Fun

Prescribing vitamins for the undernourished mom who is looking for a little joy in life

If there was ever a goal that I would die to write down on my summer goals it would be the one 17-year-old Talmadge and 15-year-old Noah had last summer: Gain 10 pounds. Just to give you the picture: Talmadge is almost 6'8", is starting to graze the tops of the door casings, and weighs 186 pounds. Noah is 6'5" and weighs 175 pounds. They have a look that's kind of a cross between a praying mantis and a daddy-long-legs. They have tried everything imaginable to gain weight. They suck in food like some of us would a chocolate shake. Once last winter Noah ate five Big Macs before dinner. And then he asked for dessert. The basketball coach has secured a firm promise that they will drink body-muscle-building shakes twice a day. In addition we try to see that they get at least four meals a day, which include thousands of calories. The grocery stores and wholesale houses love to see me pull in. The salespeople and bag boys are practically my best friends since we spend so much time together.

We have all worked so hard to help these boys accomplish their goal, but every time we got up a few extra pounds, they would play four or five back-to-back ball games expending more calories than they put in, forget to eat lunch one day and alas, at the end of the summer, Noah had lost 6 pounds, Talmadge had lost 4 pounds, and I had gained 10 pounds. Life is so unfair!

In fact, for me one of the great injustices of motherhood is the food situation. I like the part of motherhood that includes caring. But so much of that caring involves food. We fix lunches, bulk up athletes, prepare meals, provide food for needy neighbors, take treats to Young Women, horde Halloween candy, stuff turkey, and buy Christmas stocking stuffers. The cholesterol adds up as we make sugar cookies for Valentine's Day, paint Easter eggs, and prepare picnics for the Fourth of July and family reunions.

The bottom line for me is that I gain that weight that I killed myself losing the year before—over and over again. I'm sure I've lost at least a hundred pounds in my lifetime. Unfortunately, I don't get my picture in the tabloids holding an enormously gappy pair of pants three yards in front of me that I used to fit into. Drat! It's the same 5 or 10 pounds over and over again. I still fit into the same pair of pants, but it's hard to breathe in them.

Another of life's little injustices is that I can't seem to find time to exercise consistently. To me, everything else seems more important. Actually, after years of living with myself, I think I truly, in my heart of hearts, do not *want* to find time to exercise. I know everyone does not feel this way. Some mothers can't make themselves stop exercising. It makes them feel so good that they have become addicted. But it just makes me feel late. I can always think of things that I really should be doing.

I think it's because I don't have any endorphins. While I'm exercising I never get to a point where it starts to feel good. I just get hotter and hotter and I "don't sweat much for a fat girl," which adds to the problem. My mind keeps asking itself over and over, "How long until I can stop?" or "This is the longest half hour of my life!" or (when I'm jogging and on a diet and killing myself to drink 8 glasses of water a day) "I'm going to die before I find a bathroom." Having tried everything from jogging to Jane Fonda, I've pretty much decided that this is just one of my dreary trials in life.

A mother's life is the hardest one I know. Even as I was writing that sentence, I overheard a ten-year-old friend of Charity's who is here doing homework, calling home. This is how the conversation went: In a cheery little voice this adorable ten-year-old says, "Hi, Nate. Is Mom home? . . . She ran away? . . . Well, what are we going to have for dinner, then? . . . Okay, I'll wait for a while and call you later. Bye."

I couldn't help giggling out loud. This is one of the most all-together mothers I know! Aren't there lots of days when we all feel like running away from home ourselves? There are too many demands, too many hard things, too much to do.

Every week seems to bring some new trial. "If I can just get through this week," we think as we struggle with the complexities of life, "I'm going to start having fun." Amazingly, just as I wrote *that* sentence, Richard called on the phone. It was past dark and I didn't know where he was except that he had said he was going to pick up Noah after school and go on a special trek on horses up in the canyon to get a little one-on-one time with him. I thought they'd be back for dinner, but it was a beautiful fall evening and they decided to stay at our cabin overnight, even though it was a school night.

I had spent the afternoon trying to write amidst the regular mothering duties of picking up our Bulgarian "daughter" Eva, who needed a ride home from work; finding painkillers for Talmadge, who had sprained his back trying to lift too much in weight training; listening to the daily adventures of Charity and her friend about the boys who had sent them love notes that day; and I was trying to help Eli with a 10-hour project to make a collage showing the entire history of Utah, which he had known about for a week but was just beginning to work on at 9:00 P.M. and which, of course, was due tomorrow. I was seeing red when I picked up the phone.

"Well hi, dear," I said, trying to disguise my dismay. "Where are you?" In his big jolly Santa Claus voice, he said with great gusto (15-year-old Noah was obviously listening), "We're up here in the mountains, having *fun,* as *men* tend to do!" I couldn't quit laughing.

I for one get caught too often in the "Put your nose to the grindstone and suffer" mentality. Somehow, I find it hard to drop everything and just have fun. We endure one trial after another, thinking what a relief it is going to be to get through one crisis, and before we've even had a chance to catch our breath, another one rears its ugly head. On those weeks when I feel the martyr mentality creeping in, I go back to 2 Nephi 2:25, the old favorite: "and men are, that they might have joy." The first time I read that verse after becoming the mother of two tiny preschoolers and struggling with potty training and not having slept for several weeks, I became worried because I just wasn't feeling a lot of joy. Maybe Nephi didn't write men *and women* because only the dads get to have fun.

As I thought back on the joy I felt as I had just crept in on my sleeping baby and found him contentedly sucking his thumb, I realized something I remind myself of weekly. For mothers, that exhilarating feeling of joy does not always come in years or months or days. It comes in moments. And not only that. I have a *moment*, sometimes even several moments every day, when I feel joy. There's just one little catch. You have to watch for them. They don't often just present themselves to you. You have to notice that feeling. It comes when you giggle at a cute thing a child said. It happens when you gasp, "Look at that gorgeous sunset!" or when your soul is lifted with breathtaking fall colors or you enjoy the beauty of a winter blizzard. As a wise man reminded me last week, one of the best antidotes for depression is sunshine. Something about the warmth and the beauty of the outdoors brings the joy of the moment.

Fun is not just the same thing as joy, but one often leads to the other. Sometimes we have to force ourselves to have fun because we are so caught up in the martyr mentality. Richard has the hardest time making me have fun. Last week I was as stubborn as Charity when she decides she's not going to wear the dress I suggest for church. I could think of a thousand reasons why I couldn't possibly take three hours off for a little four-wheeling adventure in the spectacular fall colors of the canyons so near our home. Without a speck of sympathy for my busyness, he dragged me off to a day I will never forget. Funnily, I can't even remember what it was that day that I thought was so important.

Last week, I asked a group of mothers at an American Mothers' meeting what they worried about most. I got a long list which everyone nodded in agreement to as each was posed as a possible worry of motherhood. The last one was the one that stuck with me. "I just worry that my kids don't see me having fun," she said. "When I deal with them, it seems to always be in some sort of 'I have to do this or you have to do that' mentality. What if they decide that mother-hood looks so bleak that they don't want to be one? I need to show them more how much I love them and *love* being their mother!" It occurred to me that often leaving our children to go have some fun ourselves does them much more service than to stay home and herd them around!

One of my funnest things to do is to literally run away. It is an organized run that I call my Day Away. When I had six children under nine, I only did my Day Away once a year, but now I find I can run away a little more often. I used to go sit in my van for the day or visit the library if it was too cold. Now, with a little more money in hand, I've thought of more excit-ing places. I spend the day thinking about myself for a change. I write down things I think I need physically, spiritu-ally, emotionally, mentally, and socially. I dream about what I want to have accomplished in 10 years . . . in 5 . . . by next year. Next I think about each child. I write a few things that I've observed about each and think of each of their five facets, recording things that they need or things that I want for them as I do. Then I read or do something I want to do. It's amaz-ingly therapeutic and so fun! By the end of the 24 hours away, it never ceases to amaze me how much cuter the children have gotten. And Richard, who has usually been tending the children (although I've been known to hire a babysitter or ex-change days with a friend) is so much more sympathetic to the dilemmas of my life! It's a miracle every time!

As time goes on, I try to remember that losing weight and exercising are only parts of fulfilling my Day Away goals. (In fact, sometimes my goal is to forget about worrying about my weight for a while and not feel guilty about it. Then I really start having fun!) I try to look for "the moments" amidst the everyday trials; lo and behold, I realize that I'm experiencing joy almost every day.

The next time you feel the martyr complex settling in, try reminding yourself that you may be living in the most joyful time of your life, especially considering that you don't know what will happen next! So be of good cheer, lift up your heads, watch for those moments, and start having fun.

After twenty-seven years of being a mother and knowing that my main responsibility here on earth is not only to perfect myself just a tiny bit at a time but also to truly feel joy, I have realized that there is not a better way than being a wife and mother. Church callings come and go. Career challenges present themselves and pass. To me, living and loving the gospel and experiencing the refiner's fire as we try to teach it to our children, and then suddenly realizing the joy of seeing that *they* are the ones who are teaching us—this is one of life's greatest joys. Truly Nephi knew more than I had initially realized when he stated that all of us are here to have joy. He did not say it flippantly or to sound philosophical. He said it to let us know that we have come to earth (whether things are going well at the moment or not) to experience joy.

The challenge we leave you with, as we conclude this less than comprehensive attempt at administering some first aid, is for you and all of us to take a look at our lives and take inventory of how much joy we are experiencing daily. Though it may not seem like much today because of "extenuating circumstances," most of us will find that if we are aware and looking for it we will be surprised by the joy we feel when we begin counting our blessings. Watching for joy may be the greatest healer of all.